CONTESTATIONS

CORNELL STUDIES IN POLITICAL THEORY

A series edited by

WILLIAM E. CONNOLLY

The Anxiety of Freedom: Imagination and Individuality in Locke's Political Thought
by Uday Singh Mehta

The Inner Ocean: Individualism and Democratic Culture
by George Kateb

The Anxiety of Freedom

Imagination and Individuality in Locke's Political Thought

Uday Singh Mehta

Cornell University Press

Ithaca and London

Open access edition funded by the National Endowment for the Humanities/ Andrew W. Mellon Foundation Humanities Open Book Program.

First published 1992 by Cornell University Press

Library of Congress Cataloging-in-Publication Data

Mehta, Uday Singh.
    The anxiety of freedom : imagination and individuality in Locke's political thought / Uday Singh Mehta.
        p. cm. — (Contestations)
    Includes bibliographical references and index.
    ISBN-13: 978-0-8014-2756-5 (cloth) — ISBN-13: 978-1-5017-2638-5 (pbk.)
    1. Locke, John, 1632–1704—Contributions in political science. 2. Liberty.
3. Authority. 4. Imagination. 5. Individuality. I. Title. II. Series.
JC153.L87M44   1992
320'.01—dc20   92-8147

For Bhabhi and for Carol
in memory of and gratitude for
their inspiring friendship

Contents

viii Contents

Acknowledgments

This book is a reading of John Locke's political thought, and, because it is, I am particularly indebted to the two teachers and friends who taught me how to read—Sheldon Wolin, then at Princeton University, and the late David Lachterman, then at Swarthmore College. From both of them I learned that a text is much more than a compilation of ideas which should be distilled and held up to the scrutiny of critical gaze. From both of them I learned that the activity of reading involves straining to hear distant echoes and making them clear by an active process of imaginative mutuality. It seems fitting that in a work that focuses on the imagination I should have had the guidance of Sheldon Wolin.

While at Princeton, I benefited from the help of numerous friends. Irene Applebaum, Peter Benda, Sandra Clarke, Beenu Mahmood, Kirstie McClure, Tim Mitchell, and Helen Pringle all made valuable contributions to this project. Jeff Tulis and Anne Norton have continued, through the process of revision, to offer help, criticism, and counsel. Their contribution, as they know all too well, has been indispensable.

More recently, Hayward Alker and Steven Macedo offered challenging critiques. Ellen Immergut and Bonnie Honig provided numerous insights, especially for the introduction, and helped refashion the work. Maria Clelia Guinazu helped in numerous and timely ways. I am also deeply indebted to Eva Nagy for all her help.

Roger Haydon of Cornell University Press performed a minor miracle for this book. I am deeply grateful to him.

Joshua Cohen has read and reread more drafts of this book than either he or I care to recall. His exacting critical standards are happily matched with an intellectual generosity that is simply exemplary. He has led me to rethink a project in which I was deeply invested, and yet somehow he has made that process exhilarating.

Peter and Mary Katzenstein literally kept me going at a point when I did not think I had the physical or intellectual resources to continue. This book is evidence of their longstanding kindness and persistence. To Mary in particular I owe that special intellectual debt that stems from observing, speaking with, and listening to someone in whom ideas (and actions) are braided with deep and generous convictions.

In its original form this work owed its conception and its completion to the friendship, support, example, and faith of Yesim Arat. Through the process of revision, she has continued, despite the distance of time and space, to serve as an unerring inspiration. And finally, my debt to my wife, Tej: There are too many respects in which this work is the product of a joint effort. On every page and paragraph, I have had her advice and help. This book would not have been possible without her.

U.S.M.

Cambridge, Massachusetts

The Anxiety of Freedom

CHAPTER ONE

Introduction

The chief, if not only spur to human industry and action is *uneasiness* [of the mind].

—John Locke

The liberalism with which John Locke (1632–1704) is commonly identified has its origins in two widely shared and profoundly influential seventeenth-century assumptions: first, that human beings are by their nature free, rational, and equal; second, that they are therefore capable of murder, theft, and mayhem and are hence in mortal danger. Liberalism thus originates in ambivalence—in the need to order, if not limit, what it valorizes to be natural and emancipatory.

The commitment to constitutional government, with its authority limited by the sovereignty of the people, the emphasis on the rule of law as the means by which this authority is to be exercised, and, crucially, the identification of and protection from arbitrary abridgement of individual rights, including the right to property—these are the familiar responses, subsequently designated as liberal, to the hope and vexation that stem from these two epochal assumptions. In Locke, and more generally in the liberal tradition he has spawned, the intuitive justification for the institutions these responses define derives from the presumption that they establish determinate spheres of moral right which comport with the interests of free, rational, and equal, individuals and in so doing avert the diabolical consequences immanent in the unregulated interactions of our natural condition. Liberal politi-

I

cal institutions, one might say, are motivated and guided by the artifice of embedding the interactions among individuals within normative precincts and allowing individuals to be who they are within the constraints and possibilities of those precincts.

The defining problem of modern political philosophy, and of liberalism as a salient instance of that philosophy, is the justification of political authority and its various subsidiary institutions—an authority that is required for the stability of liberalism's normative precincts. This is so precisely because such institutions place constraints on what is taken as fundamental and natural, namely, the freedom of the individual. It is in response to this problem that the conflicts among individuals, that is, their capacity to murder and infringe on each other, are most commonly traduced as a justifying basis. Because we have interests and appetites and the acknowledged freedom to pursue such interests, and because in such pursuit we encounter others similarly motivated, and finally because such encounters can lead to violent and dire consequences, we agree, within constraints, to have our interests and freedom ordered and limited by an external authority. This is the archetypal narrative underlying the modern justification of political authority. It has a flexibility that allows it to take various forms. Interests, for instance, can be attached simply to individuals or to groups based on social and economic class, occupational commonalities, gender, ethnic associations, and various other combinations. Whatever their particular configuration, they are meant to vindicate the basic idea that a conflict of interests backed by appetites occasions the need for institutions that can ameliorate the diabolical effects of such encounters.

As a response to a historical predicament, this account captures many of the central political and social modalities of seventeenth-century England. The fact that Locke was deeply preoccupied with such sources of conflict and instability and that the political institutions he designed were meant at least in part as a redress to them is beyond credible dispute. He was writing during and in the immediate aftermath of the most turbulent and fractious years of English history: it would have been almost impossible to have remained indifferent to or complacent about the varied interests that had all but shattered the society he lived in.

Passions of the Mind

Notwithstanding the significance and reach of interests and appetites as motivators and explanators of conflict (and cooperation), they do not come close to exhausting the sources of such behavior, or of human endeavor more generally. In this book I pursue this simple insight. In contrast to the common emphasis on interests and appetites as underlying the project of liberalism, I view this project, as Locke elaborated it, as a response to cognitive concerns and specifically to a concern with the effects of the imagination and other passions associated with the mind. The contrast between the consequences of interests and the consequences of cognitive considerations is ultimately a matter of emphasis. It is not my purpose to deny the role played by the former; I am more concerned with pointing to the largely ignored significance, presence, and political implications of the latter. This contrast in emphasis does, however, have far-reaching effects on the puzzles we construct and the questions we ask of Locke, of liberalism, and of the societies most of us live in. As a single instance of such an effect, the acknowledgment of cognitive anxieties and a concern with the implications of the imagination reveal the sense and extent to which Locke is concerned not merely with settling the boundaries *between* individuals, that is, questions of peace, order, and authority, but also, while being concerned with these very questions, with settling the internal boundaries *of* individuals. In the concluding chapter of this work, I suggest that the status we accord to what we do in private—the familiar focus of privacy rights—is itself inextricably related to the status we accord to the imagination and to the way we conceptualize the human capacity to fantasize.[1] Locke is concerned not merely with individuals' interests but also with their subjective identities. As such he is, even as a political thinker or rather perhaps because he is a political thinker, concerned with a broadly psychological issue.

Underlying individual actions are a wide range of motives and dispositions, including, of course, urges that stem from capacities we do not under many circumstances feel in full control of. The elaboration of such a claim may have its fullest expression in the psychoanalytical tradition, but the basic insight that informs it is, as Freud himself emphasized, as ancient as "the poets" and a familiar feature of ordinary experience.[2] One need not invoke concepts such as the "unconscious" or deeply repressed childhood fantasies to give credence to the thought that much of human action and many of the conflicts attending it derive from passions, impulses, and drives the effects of which are made more threatening by virtue of the intractable sources from which they spring. The human capacity to imagine, to fantasize, and to treat such fantasies as real have political associations that go back at least as far as Plato's banishment of the poets from his republic.

The seventeenth century is similarly replete with the minutiae of interiority, of feelings, of autobiography, of psychologically revealing self portraits, of lonely Protestant consciences rustling

---

[1] Recently much has been written about fantasy, especially by feminist scholars. See Judith Butler, *Gender Trouble: Feminism and the Subversion of Identity* (New York: Routledge, 1990), and "The Force of Fantasy: Feminism, Mapplethorpe, and Discursive Excess," *Differences* 2 (Summer 1990), 105–25; Andrea Dworkin, *Pornography: Men Possessing Women* (New York: Seal, 1981); Jean Laplanche, "Formation of Fantasy," in *Formation of Fantasy*, ed. Victor Burgin, James Donald, and Cora Kaplan (London: Methuen, 1986). Also, Jean-Paul Sartre's *The Psychology of the Imagination* (1940; London: Methuen, 1972), though not recent, remains a classic.

[2] Sigmund Freud, *An Autobiographical Sketch*, trans. James Strachey (New York: W. W. Norton, 1952), p. 56.

with the absence of "superiors," and, perhaps most telling, of private diaries usually, as with Locke, written in cypher. Of the diary during this period Christopher Hill has said, "[it] does not put before us a single rounded personality, but a broken bundle of mirrors."[3] It was, after all, a remarkable register or balance sheet into which were compressed the details of manifold internal struggles: of indolence and ascetic self-discipline, of spiritual deviation and rectitude, of passionate and voluptuous fantasies and literal collusions or chastisements, of work done and procrastinated, of emotions experienced and suppressed—and all this recorded and scrutinized in private. The status accorded the imagination in the seventeenth and eighteenth centuries reveals it as simultaneously informing the rich efflorescence of utopian and dissenting thought and being held liable by Milton, no less, for Eve's fateful transgression.[4] It is not surprising that in times when the political, theological, and scientific mold of the past millennium was being recast, the imagination would acquire almost unprecedented prestige. And yet, precisely because it was recognized for authoring these forceful effects, it was almost immediately condemned by the further potential it was assumed to embody. In England, at least, with the seventeenth century we approach and cross that cusp before which, in Michel Foucault's words, "everyday individuality . . . remained below the threshold of description."[5]

In emphasizing interests and appetites to the exclusion of other sources of human conflict and anxiety, we risk overlooking aspects of modern individuality that give it much of its richness

[3] Christopher Hill, *Writing and Revolution in Seventeenth-Century England* (Amherst: University of Massachusetts Press, 1985), 1:259.

[4] "Assaying by his Devilish art to reach / The Organs of her Fancy, and with them forge / Illusions as he list, Phantasms and Dreams, / Or if, inspiring venom, he might taint / Th' animal spirits that from pure blood arise / Like gentle breath from Rivers pure, thence raise / At least distemper'd, discontented thoughts, / Vain hopes, inordinate desires, / Blown up with high conceit engend'ring pride"; John Milton, *Paradise Lost*, IV: 801–9.

[5] Michel Foucault, *Discipline and Punish*, trans. Alan Sheridan (New York: Vintage Books, 1979), p. 12.

and specificity and through which it is itself formed. Similarly, by viewing the basis and justification of political institutions by reference to interests and appetites, we obscure, by not acknowledging, their complex relationship with the psychological desiderata of modern individuality. And perhaps most important, by emphasizing the role of interests to the exclusion of cognitive considerations, we distort and understate the constraining effects of liberal institutions on the very individuality to which these institutions are meant to give expression.

I attempt to redress this absence, first, by elaborating the significance of certain cognitive (i.e., nonappetitive) features of human nature by displaying their manifest importance in Locke's political thought, and, second, by revealing Locke's response to the presence of these features and in the process suggesting how in Locke the broad contours of what one takes to be the individual derive from this response. To summarize, my central claim is that for Locke the coherence and stability of his liberalism depend on its capacity to foster successfully a particular self-understanding in which individuals come to view themselves as individuals, and that such a self-understanding is heavily contingent on embedding individuals within liberal institutions, including, most centrally, liberal education. Locke's view of education, despite a plethora of mundane details, is principally a response to the volatile effects he associates with the untutored or natural imagination. Above all else, it is an attempt to rein in the imagination, to anchor it in the fixity of habits, to curb its potential extravagance and depth by imbuing it with an outlook of deference to authority and social norms—in a word, to discipline and hence standardize its potential effects. Modern political philosophy since Machiavelli has often been acknowledged as emphasizing, in contrast to the ancients, the theme of political artifice, *techne*, and construction generally. I suggest how, despite the language of human *nature*, the reach of this theme includes the artificing of a particular kind of individuality.

As the term itself suggests, individuality can take various forms, and the phenomenon to which it refers can similarly be variously described. One such account is found in Albert Hirschman's important and highly suggestive book *The Passions and the Interests*. Hirschman draws attention to the emergence and acknowledgment of self-interest as a socially salutary mode of behavior by a variety of seventeenth- and eighteenth-century authors.[6] The moral and political endorsement of self-interested behavior was valorized through a contrast with the unpredictable and often violent consequences attached to the passions. Hirschman gives a fascinating account of how the old Christian association between avarice and sin was uncoupled to popularize and advocate the pursuit of self-interest. But to appreciate fully the originality of these advocates one must be clear about what they were opposing and the long-standing legacy they confronted. The preference for self-interest arose because it gave human actions a predictable and stable course in contrast to the passions, with their characteristically elusive underpinnings and volatile effects. Whereas the former encouraged a cautious attitude of calculation—balancing risks and benefits—the latter typically involved single-minded behavior with ruinous side effects. Similarly, whereas behavior governed by the interests was characteristically "cool and deliberate," the passions were widely disparaged as leading to impulsive, heated, and irrational acts. Hirschman's focus is almost exclusively on the aristocratic and militaristic passion for glory, with its ideal of conquest and its bloody effects.[7]

Despite Hirschman's rather narrow focus on glory, the point he makes regarding the passions as the mark of a particularly

[6] Albert Hirschman, *The Passions and the Interests: Political Arguments for Capitalism before Its Triumph* (Princeton: Princeton University Press, 1977).

[7] For an interesting critical discussion of Hirschman, see Stephen Holmes, "The Secret History of Self-Interest," in *Beyond Self-Interest*, ed. Jane Mansbridge (Chicago: University of Chicago Press, 1990), pp. 267–86.

subversive kind of behavior has a broader plausibility and an ancient association. Ancient and modern literature is replete with lists of specific passions such as anger, envy, and melancholy, the effects of which are singled out as conspicuous expressions of a special deformity with marked social consequences. Perhaps any generalization regarding the composition of such lists and their underlying justification is bound to be inadequate without considerable contextual support, although the salience of passions with an obvious cognitive component is revealing. Despite this important caveat, three features stand out which distinguish certain passions and explain the widespread antipathy and suspicion they have provoked at least, though not exclusively, since the seventeenth century.

There is above all the aspect of an absence of self-control. Our common parlance still captures the sense in which particular passions lead to outbursts or even moments of paralysis that are unified by the fact that they are understood to stem from an absence of deliberative intervention. Saint Augustine identifies precisely this feature in his interpretation of the fall from innocence when Adam and Eve cover their genitals. For Augustine, the shame ascribed to this moment is of secondary significance and is, in any case, explained by the fact that, having eaten from the forbidden fruit and thus splintered the unitary divine force that *informed* the world, Adam at least finds his genitals moving "on their own accord." Because that original transgression releases a force that humans beings manifest but over which they have in fact only an illusionary and partial control, Adam and Eve's disobedience expresses a hubris to which the piety and quietude of faith are the only redress. It is not surprising that sexuality and the passions associated with it should come to symbolize in the Western tradition what Foucault calls the "seismograph of . . . subjectivity."[8]

Linked to this absence of self-control is a second feature that

---

[8] M. Foucault, "Sexuality and Solitude," in *On Signs*, ed. Marshall Blonsky (Baltimore: Johns Hopkins University Press, 1985), p. 368.

underlies the impugning of various passions. Passions have an air of mystery attached to them. Unlike interests, whose justifications as motivators of human actions can be gleaned from the surface because they are acknowledged as interests only when some plausible advantage can be said to accrue from them, the passions, even though they are named and as such have a denominal identity, often designate a person only as being under the governance of an inscrutable motive. In this, the madman, the neurotic, and the divine, or at any rate the religious enthusiast, are the objects of shared suspicion.

Finally, and again closely linked with an absence of self-control, is the aspect of misguided excess. We identify passion, as the term in its common usage itself suggests, with activities and impulses in which some presumed limit is transgressed and where, as it were, the destination of the activity is either unknown, insatiable, or willfully denied. This feature is perhaps best captured by the familiar expression "to be blinded by passion."[9]

As becomes evident in Chapter 3, Locke identifies and impugns the imagination with all three of these threatening features. Still, a focus on the imagination and cognitive features more generally is largely absent in interpretations of Locke's political thought, as is a recognition of the extent of his ambivalence about the human capacities he acknowledges as natural. It is as though we have read and accepted the term "natural" with a premodern solemnity associated with dispositions and attributes chiseled in granite. Yet, it is around the very terms "nature" and "naturalness" that the most creative artifices of seventeenth- and eighteenth-century theorizing are constructed. In Bacon, Vico, Descartes, and, conspicuously, Hobbes, the term "nature" is deployed as an elaborate pun in which a concept resonant with ancient echoes of universality and necessity is serviced to promote a program replete with contingency and artifice.[10]

---

[9] The idea of passions as blinding has far-reaching importance for Hobbes. See Butler, "Force of Fantasy."

[10] The theme of naturalness and artifice inaugurates Hobbes's *Leviathan:*

It is the inculcation and consolidation of specific self-understandings, forged in response to Locke's recognition of particular features of the mind as fundamental to a stable order, that protect the determinate spheres and moral rights associated with liberalism. The profound and pervasive anxiety regarding these natural cognitive tendencies necessitates their reconstitution along with a specification of the possibilities for their expresssion. When Locke at the outset of the *Second Treatise* declares that we "must of necessity find out another rise of Government . . . [and] another Original of Political Power," he immediately follows this ambitious propaedeutic with the announcement that we must find "another way of designing and knowing the Persons" who are to have political power.[11] In light of Locke's anxieties and apprehensions pertaining to the mind, his remark regarding the need to *design* the persons who are to have political power can be seen as having literal importance.

This process of design or reconstitution is what in Chapter 4 I call the formation of individuality and it is in the course of this formation that I characterize Locke as trying to limit the acceptable forms individuality can take. At the center of Locke's theory of individuality is an emphasis on self-control and moderation, both of which are seen as derivative of the correct exercise of reason. These may very well be important virtues for individuals who, in the pursuit of their interests, run up against similar individuals. But, if the argument I am making is correct, Locke valorizes these virtues by reference to a wholly different anxiety or problematic, and they thus have a different set of effects and

---

"Nature (the Art whereby God hath made and governes the World) is by the *Art* of man, as in many other things, so in this also imitated, that it can make an Artificial Animal"; *Leviathan*, ed. C. B. Macpherson (New York: Penguin, 1968), p. 81.

[11] John Locke, *Two Treatises of Government*, 2d ed., ed. Peter Laslett (Cambridge: Cambridge University Press, 1967), p. 286. Hereafter cited as *Preface*, *First Treatise*, or *Second Treatise*.

implications—a different normative status. They are urged on individuals in response to the natural consequences of their imaginations, and hence they should be seen as attempts to delimit and mold the particular expressions of the imagination. In this response to the imagination—this attempt to regiment it, to prescribe and standardize its content, to make it submit to conventional authority—Lockean liberalism, while forming the individual, compromises his or her full potential and thus betrays an underlying conservatism.

The argument I am making is not one in which individuality is tied to a libertine imagination, to unschooled instincts, or to rationally uncontrolled urges. Nor am I proposing a Sartrean view in which the world of action is wholly determined by the possibilities of a imagined universe. [12] It is not therefore an argument against reflective and deliberative intervention in behavior. Instead my point is to show how in Locke rationality and the means for its inculcation, such as his pedagogy, function to close off forms of individual self-expression, to raise barriers against the eccentric; they are deployed to construct, consolidate, and impose a norm of "normality." In the face of motives that may be inscrutable, excessive, and singularly willful, and that may therefore issue in actions at odds with accepted and prevailing practices, Locke urges a transparency that all but requires adherence to a commonality of rather traditional norms and purposes.

What is ultimately revealing and disturbing in Locke's treatment of the imagination is that it is spurred by an anxiety about

---

[12] What I have in mind in making this comment are such remarks as the following: "It is necessary to reverse the common opinion and acknowledge that it is not the harshness of a situation or the suffering it imposes that leads people to conceive of another state of affairs in which things would be better for everybody. *It is on the day that we are able to conceive of another state of affairs, that a new light is cast on our trouble and our suffering and we decide that they are unbearable*"; Jean-Paul Sartre, *Being and Nothingness*, trans. Hazel E. Barnes (New York: Washington Square Press, 1966), pp. 434–35, emphasis added.

rather than a confidence in the potential effects of an individual's inwardness. The imagination is the expression of such inwardness; it represents a reflexivity that resists and even challenges the control and disengagement or, to use Charles Taylor's wonderfully appropriate and evocative term, the "punctuality" Locke hopes to promote and affirm.[13] This outlook underlies the puzzle of how a philosophy ostensibly committed to individual freedom and difference is transformed into an ideology of conformity with an anxious concern about individual conduct. In this book I attempt to draw out some of the implications that bear the enduring marks of the anxiety and temerity underlying Locke's affirmation of freedom and individuality.

It is a commonplace in studying Hobbes and Locke to refer to the naturalistic conceptions of human beings that underpin their political commitments. Often overlooked is the extent and manner in which these foundations have an ambivalent relation to the very political commitments they are meant to undergird. In Hobbes, the fear the sovereign inspires is an expression of both his power to coerce and his capacity to get individuals to restrain their own passions. Similarly in Locke, even though the mechanisms of restraint and the passions are different, institutions are meant to effect a change in what is taken to be the naturalistic core of human beings. In both Hobbes and Locke, and of course conspicuously in Rousseau and Hegel, political institutions fur-

---

[13] Charles Taylor, "Locke's Punctual Self," in *Sources of the Self* (Cambridge: Harvard University Press, 1989), pp. 159–76. Taylor identifies Locke with the culmination of a tradition of "inwardness" which had its greatest expression in St. Augustine. At the moment of this culmination, inwardness is transformed into a concern with disengagement and control. Taylor's chapter on Locke has several stunning and far-ranging insights, but it does, I believe, understate the extent to which Locke's thought is riddled with anxiety about those features of the mind that cannot be marshaled for purposes of control and responsibilty, such as the imagination. Judith Shklar is, I think, right when she speaks of a underlying sadness in Locke's thought, a sadness linked with "a perpetual uneasiness"; see Judith Shklar's review of *Sources of the Self* in *Political Theory* 19 (February 1991), 105–9.

nish the conditions for a transformed self-understanding—a self-understanding that buttresses political institutions as credible expressions of moral norms. The rights associated with a stable Lockean liberalism, I am suggesting, require that individuals view themselves in a specifically Lockean manner.[14] And this perspective is principally fashioned through Locke's elaborate regime for the education of young children. In this context, I am urging that we give to Locke's writings on education the same conceptual centrality that Rousseau's writings on education have long since been accorded with respect to his political thought. It is in his educational writings, the political significance of which is all but explicitly acknowledged in the *Second Treatise*, that one sees not simply Locke's ambivalence about our natural capacities and tendencies but also the degree to which these tendencies must be molded before the child is self-conscious. To put it differently, we see the extent to which the self-consciousness of the mature adult and citizen is the product of careful and detailed pedagogical crafting.

The claim that there are conditions for self-understanding must, however, in the context of Locke at least, be sharply distinguished from the postmodernist claim that there is no truth about selves independent of the way they understand themselves. Whatever tilt one gives this antiessentialism, whether in the direction of Richard Rorty's spirited and eclectic pragmatism or in the way of Gilles Deleuze's proto-Marxist affirmation of schizophrenia, it does not serve the prosaic task of interpreting Locke. John Dunn and numerous other scholars have amply confirmed that Locke's thought, notwithstanding the various

---

[14] I am indebted to Joshua Cohen for this formulation. The issue of self-understanding and its relationship to political institutions is often discussed in terms of the social bases of self-respect, which Rawls featured as an important primary good. See Joshua Cohen, "Democratic Equality," *Ethics* 99 (July 1989), 727–51; Will Kymlicka, *Liberalism, Community, and Culture* (Oxford: Clarendon Press, 1989), pp. 61–63, 192–93; and Nancy Rosenblum, *Another Liberalism* (Cambridge: Harvard University Press, 1987), especially pp. 153–86.

transitions it straddles, is firmly anchored by theological axioms that vitiate such postmodernist claims as credible interpretations.[15]

The claim that institutions have a transformative, and not merely regulative, character is a fairly commonplace one. The transformative character of political and social institutions has ancient associations. Max Weber refers to the magical significance attached to primitive contracts as instances of ancient political and even private institutions. Contracts were viewed as magical acts precisely because it was assumed that "the person would 'become' something different in quality (or status) from the quality he possessed before. Each party must thus make a new 'soul' enter his body."[16] Freud writes of "the nature of the mental change" effected in individuals by their association to a political leader, a change with transforming effects at both individual and group levels. He links this change, in an analysis suggestive both of Hobbes and of Weber's discussion of charisma, with the fear of leaders and the memory this provokes of paternal domination.[17] For Nietzsche, covenants and contracts, both ancient and modern, effect their significance in the violence and cruelty they inflict on the mind and the body—a violence registered in a deeply personal "guilt and suffering" the effects of which invariably endure beyond the terms of the covenants and contracts.[18] This widespread acknowledgment of the transformative effects of political and social institutions underscores the

[15] Chantal Mouffe and Ernesto Laclau, *Hegemony and Socialist Strategy: Towards a Radical Democratic Politics* (New York: Verso, 1985), pp. 93–145.

[16] Max Weber, *Economy and Society*, ed. Guenther Roth and Claus Wittich (Berkeley: University of California Press, 1978), 2:672.

[17] Sigmund Freud, *Group Psychology and the Analysis of the Ego*, trans. James Strachey (New York: W. W. Norton, 1959), pp. 49–50. Also see Anne Norton, *Reflections on Political Identity* (Baltimore: Johns Hopkins University Press, 1988), chaps. 3 and 4.

[18] Friedrich Nietzsche, *On the Geneology of Morals*, trans. Walter Kaufmann (New York: Random House, 1969), pp. 61–65.

need for careful attention to precisely how and in virtue of what exigency such transformations are felt and directed. In Locke, I am suggesting, political and social institutions are marshaled because of an anxiety associated with the natural cognitive tendencies of the mind. Given the nature of this anxiety and the fact that it is attached to a view regarding the mind's *natural* tendencies, it is not surprising that Locke's efforts should be directed at the infant child.

Madness and the Imagination

From a broad range of modern perspectives, as a mode of theorizing and in terms of its normative ideals, there is something self-evidently appealing even beyond the attraction that familiarity breeds about the liberal political vision, with its focused attention on human nature and its attendant requirements. It acknowledges a broad diversity of beliefs, values, dispositions, and interests and an implied plurality of life plans. It features as a central human commitment an interest in freedom, and it professes to design and justify political institutions only to the extent that they satisfy the interests of individuals conceived as free, equal, and rational.

As the expression of a historical motive, liberalism redresses the millennium and a half of Christian neglect to such human imperatives. By giving clear expression to the domain of human concerns, it disentangles them from the obscuring web of "natural hierarchies" and providential plans. And despite the teleological traces that persist in the form of substantive political constraints, despite Nietzsche's charge that they are indicative of a "*will* to self-belittlement . . . since Copernicus,"[19] this vision celebrates the triumph of human self-assertion. It brings into the

---

[19] Ibid., p. 68.

foreground a consideration of human will, capacities, preferences, and interests without resorting to the excessive philosophical paternalism and inequities of ancient Greek essentialism. In
brief, it frees human beings, in great measure by conceiving of
them as naturally free, from the medieval premise that the world
has a particular order that fully prescribes the mode of their
behavior in it.[20]

John Locke has come to represent an archetype of such theorizing. His opposition to the political absolutism of his times
and of some of his philosophical contemporaries, his endorsement of constitutional government, with the superintending assurances regarding the sovereignty of the people and the limits
that such sovereignty places on the legitimate exercise of political
authority, are all commonly viewed as having their basis in a
view of individuals as equal, free, and rational. The familiar
institutional arrangements with which he is identified all have
their putative justification in "procuring, preserving and advanc-
ing" the interest people have in "life, liberty, health and indolence of body, and the possession of outward things."[21] Like
Hobbes, Locke has come to stand for a style of theorizing that is
driven by, and receives its inspiration from, the imperatives of
human nature. The challenge of political institutions is to accommodate human beings as they are in their natural plenitude,
subject to certain normative constraints and the securing of
peace and social order.

Where political institutions emerge from and are designed
to accommodate our interests in procurement and self-
preservation, it is perhaps only to be expected that the other
expressions of our freedom evince a decorous tenacity. There is a
self-assurance to Locke's "men," with their natural rights, their

---

[20] See Hans Blumenberg, *The Legitimacy of the Modern Age*, trans. Robert M.
Wallace (Cambridge: MIT Press, 1983), pp. 181–85.

[21] John Locke, *A Letter on Toleration* (Indianapolis: Bobbs-Merrill, 1980), p. 12.

property, their natural interpretive and executive facility regarding their rights, their reason carefully trained on natural law which gives their world its moral moorings—and all this before they become citizens. Perhaps for such beings the need for political society has no greater urgency than the persistent irritant that stems from wandering into other people's turf, of getting one's interpretations of natural law entangled in juridical confusion, or the inconvenience of finding, among one's midst, the occasional miscreant with excessively possessive appetites. Perhaps for this reason Locke's political thought has so often tempted theorists and citizens with the fantasy that, with few modifications, it could be pressed into service to all but evacuate the need for any coercive regulative mechanism.[22] On this reckoning, political society may very well be, as some of Locke's formulations suggest, an elaborate procedure for defining a *primus inter pares* or, in Locke's still more undramatic terms, a "common superior" with a power and authority to settle conflicts, make and interpret laws, and incarcerate those with excessively possessive appetites.

In trying to understand this political vision, with its sober assumptions regarding human nature, it may appear that one should eschew the categories of political philosophy and instead invoke the insights of a sociological tradition that has focused on the significance of the plethora of social details that underlie such a vision and give it its self-assurance. The sobriety of political society and the citizens who inhabit it may simply be the visible veneer that conceals a complex constellation of carefully crafted and rigorously enforced social codes, duties, and obligations. The challenge, therefore, of maintaining and reproducing liberal

---

[22] The most distinguished modern exponents of this tradition are Friedrich Hayek and Robert Nozick. See Hayek, *Law, Legislation and Liberty*, vol. 1: *Rules and Order*, and *Law, Legislation and Liberty*, vol. 2: *The Mirage of Social Justice* (Chicago: University of Chicago Press, 1973, 1978); and R. Nozick, *Anarchy, State and Utopia* (New York: Oxford University Press, 1980).

societies is to be sought and understood through the cultural mores, the social conventions, the aesthetic sensibilities and, more broadly, the *habits* that quietly give such societies their stability and coherence.[23] Or perhaps in trying to understand the basis of Locke's liberalism and its political and institutional vision one should start by studying the novel, whose provenance is broadly coincident with the more philosophical and theoretical justifications of liberalism, and which, in Lionel Trilling's words, was "the most effective agent of the moral imagination" during the eighteenth and nineteenth centuries.[24] Perhaps what is implicitly presumed in a work such as Locke's *Two Treatises of Government* is the vast range of interdictions, disciplines, and restrictions to which Michel Foucault gave sustained and insightful attention. Perhaps what allows the formalisms of freedom, equality, and rationality to serve as the basis of such a complex social and political phenomenon of such enduring longevity is that these terms are merely the gloss, the caption, to a well-manicured set of latent cultural dispositions and sensibilities. Perhaps the absence of a more turbulent and contested domain to which political institutions are meant as a redress is puzzling simply because we have read Locke, literally, as a theorist and a philosopher whose pronouncements are thus presumed to have a generality, whereas in fact his thought was biographically anchored in the vision of an English gentleman with aristocratic affiliations, presuming on the accompanying assurances. Perhaps

[23] For a discussion of habits, see Norbert Elias, *The Court Society*, trans. Edmund Jephcott (New York: Pantheon, 1983), and *The Civilizing Process: Power and Civility*, vol. 2, trans. Edmund Jephcott (New York: Pantheon, 1982); and Pierre Bourdieu, *The Logic of Practice*, trans. Richard Nice (Stanford: Stanford University Press, 1990), pp. 80–97, and *Distinction: A Social Critique of the Judgment of Taste* (London: Routledge & Kegan Paul, 1984). Also see the brilliant essays "Fashion" and "Subordination and Personal Fulfillment" by Georg Simmel in *On Individuality and Social Forms*, ed. Donald N. Levine (Chicago: University of Chicago Press, 1971), pp. 294–323, 340–48.

[24] Lionel Trilling, *The Liberal Imagination* (New York: Doubleday Anchor, 1950), p. 214.

we have simply exaggerated the distance between Locke and Burke.

Even though I do not, in the main, follow these suggestions, they are not meant rhetorically. Harold Laski's comment that it is, "indeed, one of the primary characteristics of the British mind to be interested in problems of conduct rather than of thought" has a particular resonance with Locke.[25] His stature and influence as a philosopher in the eighteenth century was matched, if not rivaled, by his stature and influence as a glorified Mr. Manners.[26] Certainly Laurence Sterne's *Tristam Shandy* has a better claim than most explicitly philosophical and political interpretations as the deepest reading of Locke's conception of the imagination and the self. No work, in my view, has elaborated, albeit humorously, the anxious implications that follow from Locke's doctrine of the free association of ideas and associationist psychology more generally than Sterne's novel.

And yet, for the most part, Locke's interpreters have not focused on or even drawn attention to an underlying preoccupation with cognitive and imaginary anxieties and to the political implications that follow from these. In a sense it is easy to understand this omission and the derivative omission of a perspective that takes issues of self-understanding and self-control as central. As I have indicated, the problematic with which Locke and the tradition he spawned are linked is one in which free, rational, and equal individuals, by virtue of these capacities, invade each other's turf or, more egregiously, murder and cause mayhem. The context of the civil war and revolution in seventeenth-century England, one might assume, gives historical support to this perspective. Individuals have possessive appetites and are partial to their own interests, and thus, with or without

[25] Harold Laski, *Political Thought in England: From Locke to Bentham* (London: Oxford University Press, 1950), p. 11.

[26] See Hans Aarsleff, "Locke's Reputation in Nineteenth Century England," *Monist* 55 (1971), 409.

provocation, they are liable to incite disorder. In the presence of such possibilities and with the memory of their occurrence, one might assume, as I believe most Locke interpreters have, that the principal motive informing Locke's thought is to obviate such eventualities. To put it differently, if the problem to which Locke is thought to be responding is that political disorder is consequent to human appetites and interests, then it appears almost natural to assume that political institutions are meant as a mechanism to police precisely these appetites and interests. Furthermore, the significance of these institutions is exhausted by the extent of their success or failure in policing these appetites and interests within certain normative constraints. On this view, Locke turns out to be responding to much the same concerns Hobbes is commonly taken to address, even though Locke's response need not, by virtue of the commonality of problems, be a disguised endorsement of Hobbes's conclusions.[27]

The credibility of this general perspective turns on interests and appetites being the principal source of conflict and social disorder. It is these attributes that incline human beings to the partiality that unsettles the *society* of the state of nature and threatens to subvert it into a condition of war, thus occasioning the need for political society. Nothing beyond these attributes is implicated, and therefore one might plausibly say that the responses offered in terms of political institutions need not concern themselves with other aspects of the self. And, by implication, it

[27] I say "commonly" because the interpretations that see Hobbes as concerned exclusively with the conflict of human interests are, I believe, ultimately misguided themselves. Joshua Cohen offers a corrective to this view by emphasizing the centrality of certain passions, principally pride and honor, in "Autonomy, Security and Authority: Hobbes's Defense of Absolutism" (M.I.T.: Political Science Department). In a similar vein, William Connolly has offered an original interpretation that emphasizes the importance of cognitive considerations in Hobbes. To the best of my knowledge, he is the only scholar to recognize and feature Hobbes's discussion of madness as central to an understanding of his political thought; see William Connolly, *Political Theory and Modernity* (New York: Basil Blackwell, 1988), pp. 16–40.

may be said that issues of self-understanding have, at best, only a limited relevance—limited by the extent to which they are involved with considerations of interests and appetites.

In offering an alternative view in which self-understanding of individuals is featured and the significance of education interpreted via the role it plays in forging such a self-understanding, I am claiming that the central locus of conflict and disorder for Locke lies at a cognitive level and not at the level of interests and appetites. At the interpretive center of this book (Chapter 3) is a discussion of the imagination and specifically of madness. In contrast to a millennium and a half of theorizing about madness that identified it as a lack of Christian virtue, a mark of satanic or divine influence, or simply a form of fundamental ontological alterity, Locke views it as nothing much more than a mundane and natural feature of the imagination. Madness "has its Original in very sober and rational minds;" indeed, Locke finds it "to spring from the very same Root, and to depend on the very same Cause" as reasonableness. If it is an affliction or a condition of weakness, it is "a Weakness to which all men are . . . liable [and] which . . . universally infects mankind." As to its effects, it "is of so great [a] force to set us awry in our actions, as well Moral as Natural Passions, Reasonings, and Notions themselves, that, perhaps, there is not any one thing that deserves more to be looked after."[28] Only a thin and barely impermeable membrane tenuously holds back the sober mind from slipping into a stupor of imaginative drunkenness—a drunkenness in which, moreover, the mind is intoxicated by nothing evil, nothing exogenous, indeed nothing particularly strange, just by the imagination. Precisely because this drunken madness "springs from the very same Root" as its sober counterpart, it cannot conveniently be confined in an English equivalent of the *Hopital General*. Nor

[28] John Locke, *An Essay Concerning Human Understanding*, ed. Peter H. Nidditch (Oxford: Oxford University Press, 1975), pp. 395–97. Hereafter cited as *Essay*.

can Locke's madmen be chained in the dungeons of the eighteenth-century penitentiaries, for if they are criminals, their crime is one of which we are all guilty. And if madness is at all associated with the goblins and spirits that invade the canvas of Heironymus Bosch's *Temptation of St. Anthony*, it is only to chastise the "foolish Maid, who so often inculcates these [images] on the mind of a child" (*Essay*, p. 398). Madness, as the weakness to which all are susceptible and as the disease that universally afflicts us has become natural. It holds court at the mind's deepest core, where it challenges politics with the constant threat of an inner insurrection.

Locke invokes none of the familiar categories through which madness had been viewed. Regarding madness, he inherits, in his own view, an analogically bankrupt tradition. Despite the enormous differences in consequences attached to madness and to its opposite in terms of social order, the distinction between the two turns on nothing except cognitive self-control and its attachments. Locke's fixation—and it was that—with madness as a cognitive condition that revealed an essential kernel of liberal societies is suggested in Tocqueville's interpretation of early nineteenth-century America:

> In France we are worried about the increasing rate of suicides; in America suicides are rare, but I am told madness is commoner than anywhere else. . . . Their will resists [suicide] but reason frequently gives way. In democratic times enjoyments are more lively than in times of aristocracy. . . . But, on the other hand, one must admit that hopes and desires are much more often disappointed, minds are more *anxious* and *on edge*, and trouble is felt more keenly.[29]

Tocqueville's comment echoes Locke's concerns. The discussion of madness is a piece, perhaps the most illustrative piece, of a

[29] Alexis de Tocqueville, *Democracy in America*, trans. G. Lawrence (New York: Anchor Books, 1969), 2:538, emphasis added.

broader concern with the political centrality of the disorders of the mind. The acknowledgement of these disorders leads, I believe, to a reconsideration of other important features of Locke's thought. For instance, interpretations of Locke's views on natural law have centered around the question whether Locke believed in such laws, acknowledged their appropriately distinct and elevated status, and associated them with the traditional set of moral injunctions and restraints.[30] There is a strange scholasticism to these questions, and the contortions involved in giving them significance often belie the credibility of the responses. Locke's belief in natural laws and in such laws as constituting the moral moorings of the world strikes me as beyond credible dispute. For such laws to serve as credible moral norms, however, requires more than a belief in their existence. Clearly a belief in such laws is consistent with there being a large gap between the principles they articulate and the concrete situations in which they are to supply guidance. More important, from my perspective, the existence of such laws does not settle the issue of whether at a cognitive level human beings understand and are motivated by them. Locke believes that human beings have the *capacity* for understanding natural laws and for being motivated by such understanding and by the sanctions attached to the violation of such laws. But he is far less sanguine about human beings at a natural level actually exercising the "calm and measured" reason required for understanding and being motivated

[30] For discussions of natural law in Locke, see Leo Strauss, *Natural Right and History*, (Chicago: University of Chicago Press, 1953); John Dunn, *The Political Thought of John Locke: An Historical Account of the Argument of the "Two Treatises of Government"* (New York: Cambridge University Press, 1969), pp. 187–99; Sheldon Wolin, *Politics and Vision: Continuity and Innovation in Western Political Thought* (Boston: Little, Brown, 1960), pp. 286–351; John Finnis, *Natural Law and Natural Rights* (Oxford: Clarendon Press, 1980); Lloyd Weinreb, *Natural Law and Justice* (Cambridge: Harvard University Press, 1987); Ian Shapiro, *The Evolution of Rights in Liberal Theory* (New York: Cambridge University Press, 1986), chap. 3; Thomas Pangle, *The Spirit of Modern Republicanism* (Chicago: University of Chicago Press, 1988), chap. 13.

by natural laws. Issues pertaining to natural law in Locke are not settled at the ontological level, nor at the level of epistemic capacities; rather, I believe, their precise significance in Locke's political thought is vitiated at a cognitive level, that is, by human beings who do not stay the course even after reason has acknowledged it, and this because of the "unsteadiness" of reason. Given this fact, Locke's pedagogical project, with its focused attention on molding children's minds by making them acutely sensitive to matters of reputation and authority, has a direct bearing on the viability of natural law as a tenable normative order.

Below the Threshold: Liberals and Communitarians

In recent Anglo-American political theorizing, discussions of the self have assumed a special poignance. The critical interchange between liberals and communitarians often centers on the contrasting characterizations of the self, from which are drawn wider points of contrasts. This book was not conceived or written in light of these contemporary discussions among liberals and communitarians. It was meant, and ultimately this is all I claim for it, as an interpretive essay on Locke's political thought which selectively draws on most of Locke's major writings to illustrate a particular anxiety about the natural self that underlies them. Even within this arena, my aims are considerably narrower than many works that exclusively focus on one thinker. I do not systematically consider the progression in Locke's thought from his early *Essays on Natural Law* to his mature works, nor do I distinctly deal with his views on religion, revolution, toleration, money, language, epistemology, or metaphysics. I do not discuss the contentious issue of how best to interpret a thinker such as Locke: whether to locate him within the admittedly epochal context of seventeenth-century England as a peer to the great personages and intellectuals of his times, or as a conspiratorial pamphleteer whose concerns were mainly those of a political strategist buffeted by local constraints, or as a philosopher who wrote *sub specie aeternitatis* in the great tradition that includes Plato, Kant, and Hegel. On this latter issue, a resolute methodological indifference commits me to say nothing in advance. In any case, there is no denying that by now Locke has become an icon who sustains a polytheistic church.

Notwithstanding these denials, my argument does, I believe, in a limited manner offer a distinct perspective on the liberal-communitarian debate. Isaiah Berlin's famous "Two Concepts of Liberty" supplies a helpful way to characterize many of the issues involved in this debate. Berlin distinguishes two conceptions of liberty, negative and positive. The former, which Berlin indicates is an expressly "political liberty," defines "the area within which a man can act unobstructed by others." Echoing the argument of Mill's *On Liberty*, Berlin's principle proscribes a deliberate interference from and toward others and is hence not for the most part limited by personal capacities and talents. In contrast, the positive conception of liberty consists in being "conscious of myself as a thinking, willing, active being, bearing responsibility for my choices and able to explain them by reference to my own ideas and purposes"; in brief, it requires self-mastery and self-control, and therefore its existence or failure turns on internal grounds.[31]

The qualification in the previous paragraph—"for the most part"—is important to interpret correctly both Berlin and the liberal–communitarian debate he helps elucidate. Negative, or political, liberty is not wholly independent of human capacities and attributes. Its normative ascription is not therefore unrelated to a specification of certain human talents, even though these specifications are meant to define a minimum rather than a

[31] Isaiah Berlin, "Two Concepts of Liberty," in *Four Essays on Liberty* (Oxford: Oxford University Press, 1979), pp. 122, 131.

higher threshold. Thus, even for negative liberty Berlin specifies certain minimum conditions of rationality and deliberative competence that must be met before someone is considered politically free. Insanity, delirium, and hypnotic trance are all conditions that explicitly disqualify an agent from this freedom.[32] Put differently, even political liberty does not merely turn on the possession of certain capacities but on the actual and competent exercise of these capacities.[33]

Berlin is explicit that positive liberty requires a more richly developed set of talents and virtues, which in turn are the basis of more valuable ends, including for instance a sense of social solidarity. His point is to distinguish political freedom from a freedom that is the basis of various other valuable goods that require a higher threshold of rationality and self-control. It is the conflation of these two freedoms that Berlin is objecting to—and not to the fact that positive liberty does bring with it perhaps a richer set of ends. But both liberties are contingent and hence not absolute, they are contingent on different sets of talents requiring at a minimum a certain level of rationality. Between the talents requisite for negative freedom and those for wholly deliberative and autonomous action associated with Kant, the range is considerable and the political visions associated with this range similarly extensive.

Berlin's liberalism, like Mill's and Rawls's, and like Locke's on

[32] Isaiah Berlin, "Rationality of Value Judgments," in *Nomos*, vol. 7: *Rational Decision*, ed. C. J. Friederich (New York: New York University Press, 1964), pp. 221–23. Berlin's argument is strongly influenced by Mill, who acknowledges similar constraints on the principle of liberty. His principle applies only to "human beings in the maturity of their faculties" and to societies in which "mankind have become capable of being improved by free and equal discussion"; John Stuart Mill, "On Liberty," in *Three Essays* (Oxford: Oxford University Press, 1984), pp. 15–16.

[33] Berlin's classic essay has generated enormous critical commentary. A recent, good discussion of positive freedom which has several insights on the complex link between positive freedom and insanity, psychosis, and mental illness is Richard Flathman, *The Philosophy and Politics of Freedom* (Chicago: University of Chicago Press, 1987), especially chap. 4.

the common interpretation, is a liberalism in which the threshold of substantive conditions, including rationality, is not set so high as to be excessively exclusionary. It presumes that individuals satisfy the conditions requisite for negative liberty without demanding or expecting them not to develop the talents and life plans self-control makes possible. The challenge to this vision from communitarians such as Alasdair MacIntyre, Michael Sandel, Michael Walzer, and Charles Taylor, notwithstanding various important contrasts among them, is ultimately linked to a dissatisfaction with the conception of the self that is alleged to underlie this vision. This conception is variously characterized as "thin," "anomic," "detached," and even "devoid of character." At the root of these characterizations is an odd mix of ambivalence, rejection, and confusion about Berlin's two liberties and the liberalism he and others set out. Communitarians range between denying that the persons associated with Berlin's negative liberty are in any sense free and claiming that there exists, presumably in all or most of us, a true self that evinces the self-control and mastery associated with Berlin's positive freedom.

Taylor, for instance, accuses such liberals as Berlin of overlooking the various ways in which even the conditions for negative liberty can be obstructed by those who are neither mad, delirious, nor hypnotized. Human beings can be beset by desires they do not really identify with (desires that run contrary to their life plans and projects); they can have "inauthentic desires" and they can respond to relatively insignificant desires. For Taylor, in responding to such desires, human beings are not free: "We can experience some desires as fetters because we can experience them as not our's. . . . Desires may frustrate our deeper purposes and may be inner obstacles to freedom." Taylor's communitarianism and his critique of Berlin is an attempt to overcome "the metaphysic . . . of a higher and lower self" associated with Berlin's two liberties.[34] To this end Taylor offers what curiously

[34] Charles Taylor, "What's Wrong with Negative Liberty?" in *Philosophy and*

amounts to a metaphysic of the authentic self that has, as an underlying core, an implausible degree of internal equanimity, self-knowledge, and other cognitive assets. Free action is ultimately the action of this already empowered self.

Taylor's communitarianism is that of autonomous individuals unburdened by the hindrances of narrow, unreflective, silly, or shallow pleasures. Even when these pleasures are experienced as moments of freedom, they do not vindicate the self, a self Taylor wants to identify with actors who manifest an unerring self-reflective authenticity. There is a strange mix of psychological naivete and political ambivalence in Taylor's communitarian project. His "self," to whom the adjective "true" is appropriately added, is free not only of transient desires, facile needs, uncontrolled urges but also of spontaneity. [35] Indeed, spontaneity, which is valorized by theorists of individuality such as Nietzsche and Emerson, is seen by Taylor as the mark of a fundamental absence of self-control, discipline, and deliberation. [36] The profile of this individual appears sculpted by the hyperrationalism of a philosopher's experience. As for his political ambivalence, on the one hand Taylor denies people the right to lead what he calls truncated lives; we cannot "sensibly claim the morality of a truncated form of life for people on the grounds of defending their rights."[37] On the other hand, he does not, at least not explicitly, permit the highly interventionist measures that on his own account would be required to overcome the plethora of

---

the Human Sciences: Philosophic Papers (Cambridge: Cambridge University Press, 1985), 2:225–26, 216.

[35] Stephen Macedo, Liberal Virtues (Oxford: Oxford University Press, 1990), chap. 6. I have benefited enormously from the lucid discussion of this debate in Macedo's book. See also Kymlicka, Liberalism, Community, and Culture, and Rosenblum, Another Liberalism.

[36] See George Kateb, "Democratic Individuality and the Claims of Politics," Political Theory 14 (August 1984), 331–60. I am indebted to Bonnie Honig for suggesting this point.

[37] Taylor, "Atomism," in Philosophy and the Human Sciences, 2:199; also quoted in Macedo, Liberal Virtues.

internal obstacles that stand in the way of the self-realization of the true self.

For Sandel, the objections to liberalism derive from the gulf it opens between persons and their ends, goals, and commitments to others. It is a gulf that has its basis in the deontological presumption of individual identity that is free from the aims and attachments of individuals. For such liberals, "identity is un-problematically assured."[38] All the attributes of such identity stand at a distance from it and hence have the character of possessions.[39] In contrast to this possessive self, which stands at a distance from its attributes because it holds them as mere possessions, Sandel offers a self constituted by commitments, attachments and situations. This situated self draws its identity from the commitments and associations with which it is, in an almost literal sense, infused. In contrast to the impersonality that liberalism, according to Sandel, encourages and the distances between and within individuals it engenders, the situated self seeks its identity from "those aims and attachments from which it cannot stand apart." These constitutive attachments "become more and more *me* and less *mine*."[40]

Sandel's offers this critique to diminish the distance liberalism creates between the self and its goals and ends. In valorizing constitutive attachments, Sandel would have us discover who we are by acknowledging the attachments that make us who we are. Instead of viewing these attachments with the impersonality that needs to possess them as "mine," they are to be seen as constitutive of "me." Sandel's is a truly non-Lockean world, but it is so not so much because of what it proposes but rather what it

[38] Michael Sandel, *Liberalism and the Limits of Justice* (Cambridge: Cambridge University Press, 1982), p. 179.

[39] It is worth considering whether this view corresponds more closely to Rawls's view, as Sandel would have it, or rather to Taylor's "true self."

[40] Sandel, *Liberalism and Limits*, pp. 182, 56. See Kymlicka, *Liberalism, Community, and Culture*, for a sustained critique of the idea that one cannot stand critically apart from the allegedly constitutive attachments of the self.

presupposes—and in the critical potential it denies. Locke's individuals, one assumes, would also cherish these well-agluttenated identities that are confirmed by the knowledge of one's constitutive attachments, of one's kinship bonds and shared sentiments. But Locke's individuals, like us, though being informed and supported by these prenatal horizons, could stand apart from them, critically evaluate them, and, despite the inevitable pain and struggle involved in estranging oneself from one's inheritance, also therefore utlimately reject them.

Locke has a ubiquitous presence in the debate between liberals and communitarians. He is taken to exemplify, in its original and hence decisive form, arguments in favor of negative liberty and the detachment and impersonality ascribed to liberalism by the communitarians. My purpose here is not to challenge or defend the interpretations of Locke on the basis of which these commending and condemnatory ascriptions are made. As I have mentioned, I neither conceived nor wrote this book with this debate as its principal focus. Instead, I want to very briefly suggest the implications of my argument for the positions being debated among the liberals and communitarians and for Locke's place in this debate.

If I am correct in claiming that anxieties about cognitive disorder and madness are critical to Locke's institutional design, then clearly from the standpoint of this interpretation the idea of negative liberty understates what is involved in meeting the threshold for such liberty; if madness and delirium in the manner that Locke understands them are pervasive and mundane features of the human condition, then one needs to take more seriously than Berlin does the problem of how human beings can be made to satisfy the contingent requirements implicit for political freedom. For Locke, I believe, the correspondence between negative and positive liberty, and between political freedom and self-mastery, is ultimately untenable because self-mastery or self-control is required as a condition for negative liberty itself—

and this precisely because, at a natural level, Locke discovers a pervasive cognitive libertinage. The binary between the mad and the insane, the situated and the unsituated, the negative and the positive freedom that underlies this debate is, in Locke's work itself, a site of contestation, pedagogy, habituation, and more generally construction. This is not to deny that Locke's conception of natural freedom corresponds very closely with Berlin's negative liberty. As with Berlin, so too with Locke— natural freedom designates a specifically political freedom, and for Locke such freedom exists despite the plethora of natural obligations. I suggest, however, that there is an ambivalence in Locke's own conception of natural freedom—an ambivalence signaled by the extent and intensity of cognitive disorders Locke associates with the natural human being. A different way to put this is to suggest that the very arguments Locke offers for keeping children in a condition of tutelage before they actually become free (i.e., when they come to have reason) apply for the same reasons to adults. In making this point, I must emphasize that I am not criticizing Berlin's notion of negative liberty; rather, I am criticizing both the use of that notion as an interpretation of Locke's conception of natural freedom and also the set of curiously impoverished binary positions Berlin's initially subtle, even if problematic, distinction has given rise to.

Obscured Beginnings

Finally, I offer a word about the origins of this book. Despite the variety of current scholarly traditions that concern themselves with the self, this work was not largely inspired by them. The conscious origins of this book lie in an extravagant, perhaps naively extravagant, set of questions: could the liberal citizen be gainfully identified and understood as the neurotic of whose psychological biography Freud wrote so compellingly? Could these renunciatory demands of modern liberal citizenship bear an explanatory kinship to the repressive economy of the individual consciousness? Could these renunciatory demands perhaps have induced the repressive processes and their effects as evinced in the neurotic? And finally, if they did, what might this indicate about the normative ideals of liberalism?

Although these and related questions are tied to the conception of this work, their presence is only dimly evident in it. If these questions configure the trajectory of this book, they do so by having triggered a secondary set of concerns with which the final product is more manifestly linked. But such processes of succession are seldom neat and complete. Succession invariably leaves behind a residue, and this residue, by being left behind, does not always recede into inert inconsequence. Indeed, intellectual residues, perhaps not unlike relegated desires, often have a special poignance in establishing the coherence of their refracted and recalcitrant consequences. Origins, after all, are not merely starting blocks placed on a line; rather, as the metaphor suggests, they designate a path with a specific end and a gathered set of intentions. It is because these residual intentions, which have informed this book and yet whose presence is largely concealed in it, may ultimately be the source of this work's coherence that I begin by recounting them. As the original source of what gave this enterprise this pertinence, they may persist as the final ground of its meaning despite their obviation by a more immediate set of motives.

In suggesting that the original intentions informing this book involved exploring the possible links between Freud's understanding of neurotic behavior and the demands of liberal citizenship, I am aware of the danger of being gulled into an exercise of, at best, polemical potential. One would scarcely imagine a figure more at odds with Freud's exhilarating transgressiveness than Locke. Carlyle's famous characterization of Mill as "wiredrawn," "colorless," and "aqueous" could be taken to apply with emphasis to aspects of Locke himself. Such attributes are not likely to be elucidated under the gaze of Freud's conceptual vision. The emphatic rigidity with which Locke and much of subsequent liberal thought displaces or denies the realm of interiority, not to mention the realm of the unconscious, might be taken as a denial of the very conditions that could make a gainful bridge with Freud possible. The subtle but nevertheless strident manner in which Locke undermines conscience as a politically pertinent category similarly vitiates the credibility of a psychoanalytical reading.

These and other considerations were in fact linked to the change in the work's original plan. In the face of such widely disparate vocabularies, it was difficult to sustain the anticipated focus on a close reading of Locke's text. The interpretive concerns of a psychoanalytical approach to the individual and, more important, the intellectual idiom and style in which such concerns are expressed were liable to lead me to sidestep important matters of textual detail. Finally, there is the obvious and significant issue of the distinction between the ostensive purposes of psychoanalysis and Lockean liberalism. At the broadest level and stated rather roughly, Freud is concerned with the question of who we are and how we come to be who we are through the refracted and often oblique confrontation between desires and reality. Similarly stated, Locke and the contractarian tradition presupposes that human beings are by nature free, equal, and rational, and in light of this supposition it considers which norms and political institutions are consistent with this view of who we are. Presented as such, the two enterprises mark out and move along unmistakably distinct intellectual orbits. In fact, their distinctiveness is almost part of the mold of what we designate as the liberal contractarian tradition. With rare exceptions, notably Rousseau and more recently Rawls, the proponents of this tradition have shown a remarkably naive neglect of questions of will formation and more generally of complex and nuanced analyses of motivation. It is no exaggeration to say that an important tradition of critics of liberal contractarianism, from Nietzsche to Foucault, has been spurred by the task of compensating this neglect. Much of the fiery antipathy Nietzsche expresses toward this tradition can be gleaned from the subtitle of his book *Ecce Homo*, "How One Comes to Be Who One Is." Nevertheless, the theoretical thrust of the question how we come to be who we are is distinct from the question what institutional norms are consistent with the particular conception of who we are or who we take ourselves to be. And though these distinct enterprises can be made to serve each other, without a substantially more ambitious project they are liable to draw in differing directions.

Despite the force of these reasons, and in this case their decisive impact in reorienting this work, the conceptual connection between the understanding of neuroses and the demands of liberal citizenship have, as I have mentioned, an original priority. At the most elementary level, the connection can be presented in the following way. Liberalism is commonly accepted, starting at least with Locke, to be predicated on and committed to the rigid sequestering of the private from the political realm. The viability of this distinction underscores Locke's critique of Filmer and absolutism more generally. When Locke, at the beginning of the *Second Treatise*, sets down his conception of political power by sharply distinguishing it from "that of a *father* over his children, a *master* over his servant, a *husband* over his wife, and a *lord* over his slave," he is not merely distinguishing terms the conflation of which is essential to Filmer's patriarchal project. From the perspective of his positive enterprise, what is much more important about this initial delimitation is that it puts in place some of the necessary fences on which depends the requisite level of clarity Locke want to ascribe to the realm of the political. It is this rigidly quarantined demarcation of political space that becomes an important basis for limiting the legitimate exercise of political power.

Implied, or at least implicit, in this process of demarcation is a particular understanding of the individual as an entity whose essential integrity is not violated by such fences and who therefore can be presumed to be able to block the spillover of certain private concerns into a realm where their presence would be deemed illegitimate.

It is precisely this process of anthropological sequestering that Freud takes to be riddled with individual and social subterfuge. In challenging the viability of the external fences that for liberalism mark out the distinct precincts of human endeavor, Freud challenges the understanding of the individual that is being presupposed. The marking of distinct theoretical and anthropological provinces may, in the end, be necessary for any normative enterprise. They certainly appear so for liberalism. But it is this necessity—or if not that, at least the centrality of theorizing on the presumption of such demarcations—that Freud contests.

Finally, the Lockean contract, in the language in which it is presented, is a momentous renunciatory event. One cannot but be struck by its psychological gravity. A group of individuals, marked by a muscularity of subjective capacities, equipped by their nature with executive and interpretive plenitude and the auspicious assurance of being part of an omnipotent benefactor's plan, "give up," "quit," "resign" all that is private to fashion the security that will come from political society—and all this for the sake of interests that remain, we are told, unerringly private. It is not surprising that that great psychologist of the eighteenth century, Rousseau, should have found in this celebratory moment of unity something deeply inauthentic and ultimately even deceptive. Individuals giving up what is theirs and yet not giving it up because it remains theirs to secure what is theirs: momentous differences, momentous identities. It is not the logic of these turgid transactions that Freud would question but the implications they conceal.

Locke and the tradition he spawned have often been accused

of being antihistorical in their neglect of alternative ways of organizing political life. There is perhaps another sense to this charge. Lockean individuals are consigned to forget what they gave up, to exclude the residue of their origins, to view it as a passive loss with no mnemic trace. The unsettling effect that Rousseau, Nietzsche, and Freud have on this tradition is to remind it of the lurking proximity of the wild and obscene within it. They bring home the fact that the content of our desires, passions, and emotions are inextricably intertwined with the conditions of our self-conceptions, and these themselves implicated with our social arrangements. When Freud, with lament, speaks of the understanding of civilization and progress as required in the renunciation of instinctual urgencies, he is not endorsing libertine carnage and chaos. Instead, I believe, he is reminding us of two things: one, that even at the deepest level the content of private interests are not simply given, but rather are saturated by the most intricate and apparently illusive terms of human interdependence; the second, that such interdependence can, in the absence of extreme and daunting vigilance, quite easily constrain the instinctual energies of individual lives and, in the process, exact a price paid in individual and collective neuroses.

CHAPTER TWO

The Critique of
Scriptural Politics

Whoever hath an absolute authority to interpret any written or spoken laws, it is he who is truly the lawgiver to all intents and purposes, and not the person who first spoke or wrote them.
—Bishop Benjamin Hoadly

The first treatise of Locke's *Two Treatises of Government* has the unfortunate distinction of being, along with the latter half of the *Leviathan*, among the most neglected, indeed maligned, major portion of an otherwise celebrated and much discussed body of work in political theory. In fact, a scholarly tradition chronicles and advertises this neglect. Already in the nineteenth century, Fox Bourne, a generally sympathetic critic and biographer, found the *First Treatise* "entirely out of date" and with little to recommend it.[1] Early in the twentieth century, Harold Laski, notwithstanding his remarkable capacity to illuminate works of alleged insignificance, corroborated Fox Bourne's view, adding that the work was a "tiresome response to the historic imagination of Sir Robert Filmer."[2] Similarly, Richard Aaron, although not usually rushed in his scholarly endeavors, found the work sufficiently barren so as not to be long detained by it.[3] This list

[1] F. H. R. Bourne, *The Life of John Locke* (London, 1867), 1:169.
[2] Laski, *Political Thought in England*, p. 38.
[3] Richard Aaron, *John Locke*, 2d ed. (Oxford: Clarendon Press, 1955), p. 274.

could easily be extended into the present. The attitude it would evince is sufficiently encapsulated in Dante Germino's remark that "the *First Treatise*, which virtually no one reads anymore, is a line-by-line refutation of Filmer's tome. Tedious would be perhaps too flattering an adjective for it."[4] Clearly, Herbert Rowen's admonition almost thirty-five years ago that the *First Treatise* merits more attention has, among scholars writing in English, yet to be fully acknowledged.[5]

Some obvious and weighty reasons do underlie and inform this distinguished tradition of neglect. Most conspicuous is that interest in Locke's political thought has usually been spurred by an interest in the normative concerns that attend liberalism. Given these motivating concerns, the *Second Treatise* is clearly the principal text for their interrogation, and the *First Treatise* has apparently less, if anything, to offer. The *First Treatise* is, after all, in the main reactive, and as such it at least appears to be implicated by the narrow purview of Filmer's own concerns.

Related to the obsolescence of the *First Treatise* is the simple fact of the work's main foci. Divine grant and paternity as the basis of political sovereignty are substantive claims that are, at best, tangential to the major theoretical and concrete preoccupations of political life since at least the seventeenth century. The

[4] Dante Germino, "The Contemporary Relevance of the Classics of Political Philosophy," in *Handbook of Political Science*, ed. Fred I. Greenstein and Nelson W. Polsby (Reading, Mass.: Addison-Wesley, 1975), 1:264. Charles D. Tarlton, in "A Rope of Sand: Interpreting Locke's *First Treatise on Government*," *Historical Journal* 21, no. 1 (1978), 43–73, gives a synoptic survey of what he calls "a vicious circle of oversight, prejudgment, and caricature which has effectively prohibited detailed, structural interpretation of the *First Treatise*."

[5] Herbert H. Rowen, "A Second Thought on Locke's First Treatise," *Journal of the History of Ideas* 17 (1956), 132. In the journal literature, there are a few exceptions to this claim; see, for example, Tarlton, "A Rope of Sand," Dunn, *Political Thought of John Locke*, Pangle, *The Spirit of Modern Republicanism*, and James Tully's truly creative and synthetic work, "Governing Conduct," in *Conscience and Casuistry in Early Modern Europe*, ed. E. Leites (Cambridge: Cambridge University Press, 1986).

silencing of these Filmerian positions especially in the aftermath of the political and ecclesiastical settlement of 1688 is decisive. In the fractious working out of church, state, and crown relations, in the internecine denominational debates of the eighteenth century, in the protracted process through which the meaning of the Toleration Act was settled, in all these and virtually anything else of consequence Filmer's arguments are merely distant and inaudible embarrassments.[6] It is not surprising, then, even if ironical, that Locke's *First Treatise* in having contributed to Filmer's eclipse is by association similarly afflicted.

From a more specifically textual standpoint, the *First Treatise* is burdened by a variety of limitations that almost assure and contribute to its obsolescence. Notwithstanding the controversy regarding its date of writing, the *First Treatise* more than the *Second* appears to be an outcome of a very precise and local contextual pressure.[7] Locke himself identified the work as originating in the particular and surprising reception given Filmer's *Patriarcha*. Perhaps for reasons of his own, Locke emphasizes the dramatic effect of Filmer's work: "Had not the Gravity of the Title, and Epistle, the Picture in the Front of the Book, and the Applause that followed it, required me to believe, that the Author and the Publisher were both in earnest," he would have given it up as "another exercise of Wit" (*First Treatise*, p. 159). Filmer is clearly an author of doubtful seriousness. It appears

---

[6] See Laski, *Political Thought in England*, pp. 54–85.

[7] The classic statement of the issues surrounding the dating of Locke's two treatises remains Laslett's well-known introduction to his edited version of the *Two Treatises*. Laslett places great significance in the discovery that the *Second Treatise* was, in fact, written before the *First Treatise*. This claim appears to belie Locke's own emphasis in view of the fact that the treatises were published in their present order on at least two separate occasions, on Locke's sanction during his own lifetime. Also see Richard Ashcraft's *Revolutionary Politics and Locke's Two Treatises of Government* (Princeton: Princeton University Press, 1986), especially pp. 39–127.

that but for the circumstances surrounding his work he would have been an unworthy opponent.[8]

Finally there is the style of Locke's text, which limits its viability to a specific political and intellectual milieu. The *First Treatise* is a painfully repetitive work, a feature that suggests the intention of rhetorical effectivity rather than careful theoretical articulation. It is a response to what Locke believes are ultimately mischievous interests and which must therefore, at least in part, be countered with polemical flair. Locke creates an atmosphere of sophistic combat in which his adversary is entangled in shreds of his own verbiage. When Locke strays from this style, he does so only to settle into an arcane form of scriptural hermeneutics in which citations of chapter and verse are marshaled in the manner of scholastic disputation. And all this in a work that ends in midsentence, and in which the missing section is acknowledged to be "more than all the rest" (*Preface*, p. 155).

Clearly, the scholarly tradition of neglect has much with which to justify its omission of the *First Treatise*. Indeed, the onus of justification appears to lie with those who, in the face of such reasons, insist on its theoretical significance, both as a worthy if not a necessary precursor to its more studied successor and for the broader role it plays in the understanding of Locke's political and moral thought. It is to these reasons that I turn.

Scriptural Politics: An Underlying Discourse

The confrontation taken up in the *First Treatise* is plainly of fundamental and foundational significance. At the broadest level

---

[8] My point here is simply that Locke presents Filmer in such a doubtful light. This view, as with so much else in the *First Treatise*, is repeatedly emphasized in the preface and the first few chapters. My claim, therefore, is not meant as a challenge to Gordon Schochet, Mark Goldie, and Richard Ashcraft, all of whom have persuasively argued that Filmer's theory was an important, perhaps

it involves two uncompromisingly conflicting visions of the origins and basis of political power and authority, the status of fatherhood and the family, the role and significance of property, and the relationships among property, paternity, and authority. Despite the degree to which, in Locke's view, Filmer's motives may be impugned by expedience, his doctrine incoherently presented, and its implications irredeemably contradictory, nevertheless Filmer does in a systematic manner deny the view that human beings are naturally free and that therefore there is a limit to the legitimate authority that fathers, property holders, and governments can have over them. By braiding together monarchy, paternity, and property and giving them, as Locke emphasizes, an inescapable and extensive reach, Filmer conflates the very terms around which Locke places demarcating and limiting fences. Filmer's views in a general sense sustain the edifice of feudal authority relations. Hence, notwithstanding the plausibility of the reasons that make the *First Treatise* appear puzzling and of questionable significance, if considered in terms of the issues at stake it is of unquestionable gravity.

But there is a danger in viewing the *First Treatise* as merely the stage on which this precise confrontation on issues of sovereignty, paternity, and property occurs. Despite the stakes attending these issues, if they alone are allowed to determine our view on the *First Treatise*, we are liable to overlook its multifarious echoes and to recognize their collective significance. We are liable to overlook, not only that the conception of political power Locke articulates at the outset of the *Second Treatise* is different in its specifics and implications from Filmer's conception, but that this difference stems from a more general divergence regarding the appropriate language, context, and method

even principal, source of royal absolutist doctrines during the seventeenth century. See Gordon Schochet, *Patriarchalism in Political Thought* (New York: Basic Books, 1975); Mark Goldie, "John Locke and Anglican Royalism," *Political Studies* 31 (1983), 86–102; Ashcraft, *Revolutionary Politics*, pp. 181–227.

for arguing about political issues. Similarly, we are liable to overlook that the individual Locke has in mind in the *Second Treatise* is one who emerges from and is an integral part of a broader commitment to a particular kind of narrative—a narrative in which a certain kind of information is featured and other kinds deemphasized, narrative that signifies not only an alternative conception of political power but also, and again, a distinct way of discoursing about politics. Even if one considers the *First Treatise* as merely a polemic centering on concerns most of which no longer command our interests, it still gives us a view on the terms through which Locke in particular frames his own more proximate concerns.

In emphasizing a deeper level of contestation between Filmer and Locke which turns on issues of language, history, and narrative, I am not simply making a claim for greater literary sensitivity. More important is that attention to such issues reveals substantive political concerns regarding the cognitive dimensions and more broadly the psychological identity of the Lockean individual. The significance of these concerns is, I believe, muffled if the *First Treatise* is viewed either as simply a polemical sortie with a reactionary absolutist discourse or as a staged confrontation with older notions of sovereignty, paternity, and property.

Although the *First Treatise* clearly supports both interpretations, it also, though less conspicuously, gives us an important preliminary view on Locke's perspective on the individual. It helps us understand what for Locke are the relevant cognitive and attitudinal dispositions of the individual, the psychological information appropriate to appreciating such dispositions, and the normative directives occasioned by this individual. At the broadest level, Locke's dispute with Filmer is about the origins and justification of political power. At this level, Locke's divergence from Filmer involves sequestering political power from its alleged biblical origins and the implied legitimacy. In view of the scriptural details that abound in the *First Treatise*, it is tempting to view this sequestering as stemming wholly from Locke's alternative interpretation of the Bible. In a sense, this is of course true. But one must go beyond this to inquire if Locke's view on the Bible and its relation to political power is not itself informed by more contemporaneous political and psychological insights that invite, if not require, such a sequestering. Pursuant to this view, my purpose in this chapter is to consider if underlying Locke's more familiar objections to Filmer there exist concerns that derive from aspects of the individual condition that require a distinct discourse precisely because in Filmer's conceptualization the full significance of these aspects is suppressed, truncated, or distorted.

Such expectations of the *First Treatise* may be taken as requiring the concession of shelving its more straightforward meaning and the foundational and political contrast between Locke and Filmer's positions. There are, I believe, several prima facie reasons for granting such a concession. Most obvious, it is a work whose style is so strikingly at odds with the *Second Treatise* and, indeed, with most other of Locke's works. Locke's ordinarily prosaic and plodding style is almost entirely absent. Instead, we find him flailing Filmer with a rhetorical and polemical fire reminiscent of Hobbes's more excited prose. Locke's literary posture ranges between claims of disbelief, acerbic sarcasm, closely argued syllogistic rebuttals, philological reinterpretations of the Bible, professions of piety, and indignant outrage. Even though he does present an internal and systematic critique of Filmer's patriarchal and property-based arguments, stylistically the *First Treatise* suggests that more is involved. The deployment of such disparate textual styles at least hints at the existence of an intellectual agenda that cannot be subsumed by reference to the critique of Filmer's conception of paternal power and property.

Beyond these stylistic features is the fact that, barring only Book III of the *Essay*, nowhere is Locke more explicitly troubled by issues of language and its appropriate usage. With repeated emphasis, Locke draws the reader's attention to the peculiarity of Filmer's use of words. Apart from the inaugural claim in which he tells us that he would have mistaken Filmer's *Patriarcha* as a work of "wit" but for the accompanying "noise," we are told that Filmer "cross[es] the Rules of language," that his "way of writing [involves] huddling several Suppositions together, and that in doubtful and general terms makes such a medley and confusion, that it is impossible to show his mistakes" (*First Treatise*, pp. 191, 173).[9] Further along in the *Treatise*, Locke makes the telling comment again with reference to the *Patriarcha* that it is "not by the Force of Arguments and Opposition, but the Intricacy of the Words" that Filmer's work acquires its peculiar tenacity (p. 174). These and similar references should not be mistaken as Locke's way of referring to Filmer as using nonsensical language. If it were nonsense, it would not provoke Locke to the extent it does, nor would it elicit the considerable labor Locke puts into his response. Similarly, even though Locke's chastisements may be part of his more straightforward objections to Filmer's arguments, they are not simply that. Issues of style and language point to a particular and cognitively significant source of Filmer's effectivity and a corresponding need on Locke's part to engage Filmer at this level.

Locke's critique of paternal authority and property as the basis of sovereignty is only a salient part of this larger critical enterprise. I refer to this larger endeavor as Locke's critique of scriptural politics. I view the *First Treatise* as neutralizing a way of theorizing about human beings and the institutions that govern them. In the course of this neutralization, a new set of theoretical parameters are revealed which, by the *Second Treatise*, acquire such familiarity that one is liable to overlook the various strategic

---

[9] Evidence of Locke's discomfort with Filmer's language is scattered all through the *First Treatise*. See, for example, sections 6, 7, 9, 11, 18, 19.

maneuvers that were involved in their articulation. Moreover, it becomes clear in the course of this neutralization that Locke is not only challenging Filmer's absolutism but also reconstituting the parameters of theorizing to facilitate the recognition of certain underlying cognitive and psychological features.

My reason for speaking in terms of a "way of theorizing" is to distinguish this from the more specific content and position of Filmer's patriarchalist and Adamic property-based theory. Such a distinction is important because I want to argue that Locke is in fact going beyond the precise terms of Filmer's specific theory, uncovering and neutralizing the broader norms that govern it. I hope in the course of this chapter to clarify the manner of Locke's act of theoretical displacement and the ensuing articulation of an alternative set of theoretical concerns, primarily those occasioned by the emergence of novel cognitive and psychological stirrings.

There is an obvious sense in which Filmer's doctrines express a form of political absolutism. They place no limit on the legitimate exercise of political power, imply a correspondingly extensive obligation over those on whom it is exercised, and identify the basis of this power and obligation in the inescapable fact of paternity and the divine grant of property. This view is supported by and emerges from the claim that paternity confers absolute power, and paternity therefore is effectively synonymous with the absolute rights Filmer associates with having property. To this form of absolutism, theological absolutism may initially appear only to add a clarification of the source of such authority and certain rules pertaining to its transmission. Thus, for instance, on Filmer's account, divine grant to Adam along with the rule of male primogeniture specify the terms of the original and enduring basis of political authority. Viewed as such, the distinction between political absolutism and theological absolutism appears simply in the authorizing original source. But it is precisely this authorizing source that is crucial to

Locke's critique of Filmer's political doctrines, and therefore critical to what I have called scriptural politics.

By scriptural politics I mean an orientation toward at least the political arrangements of society in which the terms of these arrangements are defined by reference to a body of knowledge that is presumed to be absolutely true and hence authoritative. There are two relevant and important implications of scriptural politics thus conceived. First, since political arrangements are derivative of a presumed body of knowledge, these arrangements need not bear any relation to the form political institutions have actually assumed in the course of human history. The fact that human beings have perhaps politically organized themselves in ways that are at odds with those prescribed by such an orientation is largely a matter of indifference to the adherents of this orientation. Because the authority informing scriptural politics is that of absolute truth, scriptural politics abjures history and relatedly abjures the need for events to have the spatiotemporal order and coherence associated with historical events. This claim is quite distinct from the claim that scriptural politics is indifferent to human events. The concern of scriptural politics with such events is testified to by the fact that it professes to know, in advance, the precise form that political (and perhaps other) arrangements should take. Its indifference lies in its being unmoved by the actual turn of events, by extant traditions of practice, and by the intimations and tendencies that are revealed by the past and that guide and constrain the present. To put it in Oakeshottian terms, scriptural politics is knowledge in advance of the activity of politics.[10]

The second relevant implication is that the orientation of scriptural politics, for the reasons stated above, is again largely indif-

---

[10] Michael Oakeshott, *Rationalism in Politics* (London: Methuen, 1962). See in particular the chapters "Rationalism in Politics," pp. 1–36, and "Political Education," pp. 111–36.

ferent to the particular needs, dispositions, cognitive makeup and tendencies, and self-definitions of human beings. None of these affect the normative ideals of scriptural politics, which are wholly derivative of the elevated veracity of its authorizing source. Thus, the issue of consent as informing the legitimacy of political institutions is wholly tangential to the perspective of scriptural politics. Finally, scriptural politics expresses an outlook on the world in which the world should be governed by a single aletheic source, and hence it expresses a fundamental connectedness of the world. To this extent, it would not be surprising to discover that various domains of authority, such as the family, the polity, and the economy, are all merely isomorphic instances infused by the same ultimate authority.

In contrasting the underlying basis of scriptural politics with history, I mean to draw attention to what I believe is ultimately crucial to Locke's critique—namely, the contrast between an authorizing source (as Locke would say, "the original") that is free of specifications of time and space and an authorizing source that is embedded within and hence constrained by such contextual specifications. Locke's critique of Filmer and the style of theorizing he represents can be thought of as an insistent demand for a particular kind of narrative in which doctrinal claims are made to cohere with spatial and temporal credibilities. In terms of the way of arguing, the contrast between Filmer and Locke is that between a discourse of truth which, because it is that, requires no supplementary narrative, and a discourse which draws its authority inter alia from the narrative coherence it can give historical events involving people with a credible cognitive and psychological profile. Locke's critique pressures Filmer into offering a narrative, or rather an interpretation, of the biblical narratives which comports with the doctrinal positions he espouses. It is precisely such an interpretation to which Filmer feels no obligation. Like the biblical narrator, Filmer is constrained by the truth of a pious and authoritative tradition and not by the need to create the impression of narrative realism. The stories of the Bible do not have to flatter our aesthetic sensibilities or perceptual expectations to validate the authority of their origins.[11] In a like manner, Filmer's way of arguing eschews the expectations and demands of people "now on Earth." For Filmer, like the narrator of the Bible, the domain of history is inextricably infused with a normative authority and, for that very reason, history is not an independent evidentiary basis for validating that authority.

While writing of the narrator of the Old Testament in his celebrated work *Mimesis*, Erich Auerbach suggests what I am urging regarding scriptural politics and its relationship to history: "The world of the Scripture stories is not satisfied with claiming to be a historically true reality—it insists that it is the only real world, is destined for autocracy. All other scenes, issues, and ordinances have no right to appear independently of it."[12] Locke's critique of scriptural politics is an attempt to break up the unity of Filmer's world by establishing the independence of various distinct precincts of authority. The literary strategy (in being literary, it is no less motivated by a theoretical and political imperative) of demanding narratives or contextual specifications serves to objectify a given domain, and this, as Charles

[11] In thinking about Locke's critique of Filmer and the distinct styles of theorizing they represent, I have found Erich Auerbach's discussion of the differences between the Homeric and the Old Testament styles extremely helpful. He characterizes these two styles as "on the one hand fully externalized description, uniform illumination, uninterrupted discussion, free expression, all events in the foreground, displaying unmistakable meanings, few elements of historical development and of psychological perspective; on the other hand, certain parts brought into high relief, others left obscure, abruptness, suggestive influence of the unexpressed, background quality, multiplicity of meanings and the need for interpretation, universal-historical claims, development of the concept of historically becoming, and preoccupation with the problematic"; Erich Auerbach, *Mimesis: The Representation of Reality in Western Literature*, trans. W. R. Trask (Princeton: Princeton University Press, 1974), p. 23.

[12] Ibid., pp. 14–15.

Taylor suggests of Descartes and Locke, deprives it of its normative force.[13]

As I have said, in the course of demanding such a narrative, with the attending specifications of time and place, the parameters of Locke's own style of theorizing emerge. These parameters reveal the dimensions of a new individual with a cognitive and psychological identity which structure Locke's theoretical efforts in the *Second Treatise*. Therefore, in the next three sections of this chapter I focus on the link between the pressing of such a narrative and the critique of scriptural politics; then, in the final section I consider, in a preliminary manner, aspects of the self revealed by this critique.

Prescribing the Context

Perhaps the most striking initial impression of the *Two Treatises* is the precision with which its author identifies the purpose for which it was written and thus situates the work with respect to an unequivocal contextual pressure. Having explained that the text is missing its middle, Locke goes on to tell the reader that "these [papers], which remain, I hope are sufficient to establish the Throne of Our Great Restorer, Our present King William; to make good his Title, in the Consent of the people, which being the only one of all lawful Governments" (*Preface*, p. 155). What is significant is not whether this expression of Locke's purposes is in fact true or whether these intentions are in fact carried out in the course of the *Two Treatises;* rather, these purported intentions suggest the constraints within which Locke places the act of his theorizing. The *Two Treatises* is *presented* as being a response and

[13] Charles Taylor, *Sources of the Self*, p. 160, also chaps. 8 and 9. Hans Blumenberg is, I think, referring to much the same phenomenon when he speaks of the "disappearance of order" in *Legitimacy of the Modern Age*, p. 137.

support to a specific political and historical event. Furthermore, a precise disposition toward this event gives the work its ostensible urgency and purpose. The event, by dating itself, further situates and circumscribes the position of the theorist. [14] Locke's own response to the now visibly demarcated context is similarly defined. It is his "hope" that his incomplete text is "sufficient to establish the Throne." His enterprise is given significance by the fact that its success will "justifie to the world and the People of England . . . their Resolution to preserve . . . the Nation when it was on the very brink of Slavery and Ruine." If his efforts are successful, "if these Papers have that evidence" (evidence enough to establish the throne), the absence of the missing middle will be no great loss. (p. 155).

Locke's use of words such as "sufficient," "justify," and "evidence" is unmistakably instrumental. They orient the theoretical activity toward a specific contextual event, and in doing so they render contingent the basis of theorizing and hence the very claims of theory. Put differently, the precise identification of the event toward which Locke's claims are directed and by which they are inspired limits the perimeter within which these claims must operate. Locke's beginning is thus deeply situated within a narrative of contemporary events—events that one must assume have widespread currency.

Instead of the more familiar theoretical stance, sub specie aeternitatis, Locke's theoretical efforts are framed with reference to the looming and contextually specific background of monumental political events. The contrast involved here is dramatized by placing Locke alongside his near contemporaries in the seventeenth century, a century famously replete with confident theoretical pronouncements of the absolute beginning of the modern

---

[14] From this perspective, it matters little that the bulk of the *Two Treatises* may have been written a decade before the revolution of 1688. My own interest, as I have mentioned, is limited by the text as it is publicly manifested.

age. Descartes' idea of a philosophy that emerges autonomously from the claims of reason and is utterly free of presupposition only mirrors his painstaking efforts to efface and deny any traces of historical dependence. His refusal to acknowledge his crucial encounter with Isaak Beeckmann in 1618 and his debt to Augustine for the argument of the *cogito* emphasize the self-conscious centrality given the notion of a philosophical sovereignty unmarked by historical dependence. Descartes' self-proclaimed designation as the originating "father of geometry," like Hobbes's characterization of "civil philosophy" as no older than his own *De Cive*,[15] is a self-interpretation that encapsulates an attitude of theoretical disenchantment with history.

It would be misleading to view such remarks as the anxious expressions of men who were either uncertain of or obsessed with their own originality. It is more important that such claims are the very expressions of a radical freedom that refuses to submit to the historical conditions under which reason finds itself. The radically novel potential of reason lay in its very capacity to present these conditions for itself. Hobbes, for instance, speaks of philosophy as "the child of . . . your own mind," and its "method must resemble that of the creation;"[16] when he does make poignant reference to his work being "occasioned by the disorders of the present time," he does so not in the preface or introduction but rather in the concluding paragraph of the *Leviathan*. Similarly, Descartes, "without wanting to offer any remarks on the employments of others," will only acknowledge "the Method which [he] had prescribed to [him]self."[17]

---

[15] Thomas Hobbes, *The English Works*, ed. Sir William Molesworth (London: 1839), 1:ix.

[16] Ibid., 1:13.

[17] René Descartes, "Discourse on Method," in *The Method, Meditations and Philosophy of Descartes*, ed. and trans. John Veitch (New York: Tudor, 1937), p. 167. Also see Sheldon Wolin, "Political Theory as a Vocation," *American Political Science Review* 63, no. 4 (1969), 1067.

In Descartes and Hobbes, one might say, modern philosophy is launched in self-conscious defiance of a dialogical structure without any need of interlocutory partners and with an expressed denial of theoretical and contemporaneous constraints. The self-image of philosophy set in the picture of Socrates unceasingly engaged in conversation, which endures in the apostolic commitment to the laity, through to the holy man of late antiquity flocked by laymen, is finally displaced by the textually sealed act of clear thinking. In contrast, we have Locke pretending to the status of King William's amanuensis and railing against a man "long since past answering."

Locke's theoretical self-restriction sets the tone for a general characterization of the critique of Filmer on which he is embarking. Locke will "endeavor to reduce his [Filmer's] Words to direct, positive, intelligible Propositions, and then compare them one with another." In the course of this, he will reveal Filmer's lack of "consisten[cy] with himself" and his deviation from common sense (*Preface*, pp. 155–56). The reference to common sense, here and elsewhere, is important. Locke persistently points to the manner in which Filmer's ideas are unable to make sense of common and well-established sensibilities. Thus, for instance, when challenging Filmer's identification of fatherly authority with monarchy, Locke wants to know if this view comports with the way "Children imagine of their Parents, or subjects of their Kings" (*First Treatise*, p. 164). Similarly, Locke points to the manner in which Filmer's "Divine Right" undermines the foundations of all existing governments, including those with a monarchical structure. (pp. 160–61). Even within the preface there is a double irony when, having identified Filmer's ideas as "his wonderful System," Locke follows this reference with "the King, and Body of the Nation, have since so thoroughly confuted his [Filmer's] Hypothesis." The rhetorical impact of Locke's rejoinder is that a historical event involving the return of a monarch suffices to undo a system of ideas that professes a particularly expansive form of monarchy. It is Filmer's inability to recognize the rationality of what is real that underlies Locke's frequent demand for evidence, reasons, arguments, proofs, and consistency.

The theme of Locke's identification with a particular historical event is given a clearer contrast in the first chapter of the *First Treatise*, where he comes to characterize the source and economy of Filmer's claims. Speaking of the *Patriarcha*, Locke says:

> This Treatise, which has lain dormant so long, was, when it appeared in the world, to carry by strength of its Arguments, all Liberty out of it; and that from henceforth our Author's short Model was to be the Pattern on the Mount, and the perfect standard of Politics for the future. His System lies in little compass, 'tis no more than this,
> *That all government is Absolute Monarchy.*
> And the Ground he builds on, is this,
> *That no Man is Born free.* (P. 160)

Let us consider Locke's language carefully. The first part of this statement introduces the central political theme Locke reiterates during the *First Treatise:* Filmer's arguments, if realized, would deprive all men and women of even the slightest semblance of liberty. In short, they would effectively chain all human beings, and "Chains are but an ill wearing, how much Care soever hath been taken to file and polish them" (p. 159). The second part of the quoted statement is not as obviously intelligible. Let us start by considering what qualification is intended by the adjective "short" to the noun "Model," for syntactically at least Locke links the carrying away of all liberty with Filmer's short model. Locke's concern with the brevity of Filmer's system is again, in the very next line, drawn out by the phrase "His System lies in a little compass." In both sentences the aspect of brevity is associated with the words "Model" and "System." Two paragraphs later, while characterizing Filmer's arguments as "fashionable," Locke again rebukes his "short System of Politics" (p. 161).

What sense are we to give to this curious emphasis on Filmer's systemic conciseness? Is there something about models and systems of politics which, by focusing on theoretical parsimony, does violence to an alternative conception Locke is trying to adumbrate? Is the concision of Filmer's system linked with the authoritative features underlying what I have called scriptural politics? These questions are neither asked nor explicitly answered by Locke. Yet his language is instructively suggestive. Filmer's short model is, of course, the Ten Commandments delivered to Moses at Sinai. But in Locke's characterization of them they are not presented as the momentous covenant between God and humanity, but rather as a "Pattern" that Filmer would have as a "perfect Standard of Politics for the Future." Neither the veracity of the Decalogue nor its monumental symbolic and theological significance is brought into question. Rather, Filmer's alleged belief in the Commandments as perfect standards for any future politics is being attacked. Such a standard circumvents the need to consider the contingency and conditional status of historical events including, of course, the conditions that circumscribe the will and consent of human beings. Put differently, Locke is challenging the fashionable urge to model politics by reducing it to some essential axiomatic core.

This core of axioms, as the generating principle, controls future politics by settling the significance of past and future events (i.e., history) and thus undermining their potential political valency. Like a set of mathematical (i.e., literally known in advance) premises, such a core of politico-theological axioms controls the theoretical conclusions derived from it. And, as in mathematics, the fewer the premises the more powerful the system. Filmer's short model is indeed economical; it requires merely scriptural evidence for a divine grant to Adam and an absolutist view of the power implied in such a grant, and it has a supplementary claim regarding the political obligations to fathers that follow from the mere fact of birth. Adam's global property claim, combined with his paternal rights, implies "that all Government is absolute Monarchy." As a model or normative ideal, it vacates the complexity of historical events, erases the spatial and temporal boundaries through which such events acquire their specificity, and instead designates a monumental beginning through which all future events are settled. Within Filmer's model, the challenge presented by historical events is simply one of fitting them into the frame of the model. In this it recapitulates the challenge faced by the early Christian church fathers in settling the status of the Jewish tradition or in assigning a proper place to the Roman Empire in the providential plan.

It may be objected that my interpretation of this passage burdens the text with unduly complex pretensions. The mention of "Short Model," "Pattern," and other such terms may, after all, be Locke's concise and systematic portrayal of the core of Filmer's views; by implication, these references may have nothing to do with a theoretical style that slights the contingencies of history and vitiates the narrative fluidity of events. It might, as part of this alternative interpretation, be pointed out that when Locke says, following his reference to "Short Model" and "System," that "tis no more but this," he suggests precisely this alternative reading. Obviously, the interpretation I am offering cannot rest simply on this single passage, especially in the face of a plausible alternative. If the passage has the significance I am ascribing to it, it must be evident as a more persistent concern. Nevertheless, even within the more immediate textual context, the theme of Filmer's slighting of history is echoed. For instance, in the paragraph immediately following the one under consideration, Locke, after making explicit reference to a generation of men who have sprung up in "this last age," elaborates on their flattery of princes by pointing to the manner in which they have encouraged a view of absolute power that is unmindful of "the laws by which they are constituted and are to govern, and the *Conditions* under which they enter upon their Authority . . . and their Engagements to observe them never so well ratified by solemn oaths and promises" (p. 160, emphasis added). The implications of this historically disengaged perspective extend beyond "Tyranny and Oppression." In fact, as Locke points out, this perspective unsettles and shakes the thrones of existing princes by implying their own subjection to Adam's rightful heir.

The contrast I am suggesting between Locke and Filmer is one between a theory that situates itself with respect to an immediate historical event of undeniable appeal and significance (the establishing of the throne of "our present King William") and one that derives its enduring authority from a context both temporally and spatially distant, indeed historically inaccessible. Filmer's absolutism is twofold; not only does he expressly endorse politically absolutist values and institutions, he also affirms what one might call, with reference to scriptural politics, a methodological absolutism—an absolutism that stems from the very denial of the historicity of politics and theory. As a critique of the latter, Locke, I have suggested, draws attention to the historically disengaged perspective that informs Filmer's way of arguing. To be systematic and authoritative in this manner, Filmer must externalize the governing core of politics from historical discourse; to have a perfect standard for all political situations, this standard must stand apart from any given political situation. Finally, Filmer's dual absolutism must freeze individuals in a perspective that denies the very possibilities of their psychological stirrings.

Paternity and Property

The substantive claims regarding history and context are also evident in Locke's more familiar critique of Filmer's political absolutism. Despite the fact that Locke's objections to Filmer's political absolutism are motivated by a more obvious set of political stakes, his challenge to Filmer's monarchist views and to the support Filmer offers for them evinces the same demand for narrative and historical coherence. It is to this confrontation that I now turn.

At the core of Filmer's political absolutism is a doctrine that obliges subjects to the authority of absolute monarchs. In Locke's characterization of this "Great Position," Filmer is said to offer two broad lines of justification. The first is the claim that God invested Adam with sovereign political authority over his children, and that this authority was transmitted by the rule of male primogeniture. Thus, the simple fact of birth brought with it an unlimited political authority and a corresponding and inescapable servitude. The ultimate justification for this view is alleged to be the scriptural injunctions that command children to obey (*First Treatise*, pp. 201–204), the medical and moral thesis that "Fathers have a Power over the Lives of their Children, because they give them Life and Being (p. 196), and finally the historical record of fathers having actually exercised such power over their children (pp. 198–201). This three-pronged justification implies and emphasizes Filmer's claims of the impossibility of natural freedom and the inescapability of royal and patriarchal absolutism.

The second line of justification derives from the notion that God, in giving the world to Adam as his private dominion, thereby invested him with sovereignty over the world. Property, for Filmer, implies an absolute political claim. Thus in having, on the basis of divine grant, property of the whole world, Adam had an absolute political claim over the world. The claim has a clear spatial and temporal referent, for it extends to the entire world and originates in the beginning of time.

Locke's objections to both the claim of paternal political authority and the private dominion argument are familiar, even to the tradition of scholars who have for the most part overlooked the *First Treatise*. Locke repeats his objections, at least in abbreviated form, in the *Second Treatise*, and in any case they can be gleaned from his own normative concerns. I rather summarily recount these objections before considering the theme of narrative and historicity, which underlies these objections though in a less conspicuous manner.

Locke's most insistent objection is to the peculiar and partial manner in which Filmer interprets scripture. With reference to the claim that scripture commands the obedience of children to their fathers, Locke emphatically and repeatedly recalls that the injunction of the Fifth Commandment includes honoring and obeying both parents (pp. 163, 189–94). In challenging the view that God gave the world to Adam, Locke mentions both the absence of such a grant with the political implications Filmer ascribes to it and the fact that the Donation was made without the specification of proper names, in the presence of both Adam and Eve (p. 179). In response to the medical and moral thesis, Locke points out that, following "the Act of Generation" as soon as "the Father has done his part," the "yet unformed Embrio" must be presumed to "owe most to the mother" (p. 198). If creation gives political authority, it therefore does so in greater share to Eve, and presumably to mothers generally. Of course, the more important objection is that neither parent has the political authority Filmer associates with birth, since God, and not parents, creates "the living soul." Locke plainly dismisses Filmer's invocation of the historical record of fathers exercising political power over their children, on grounds that such a record is unpersuasive and, in any case, irrelevant to the issue of moral justification.

The normative thrust of Locke's response to Filmer's two lines of argument is a suggestion that the power associated with neither paternity nor property corresponds to political power, with its distinctive feature of being "a Right of making Laws with Penalties of Death" (*Second Treatise*, p. 286). Anticipating a claim emphasized in the *Second Treatise*, Locke limits in time and scope the authority associated with parents and property holders. Parents have authority only before their children come to have reason and are thus capable of understanding the precepts of natural law. Even during this brief period, parental authority is limited in scope because, unlike political authority, it does not extend to the power of life and death. Similarly, notwithstanding Locke's claim that the world was not given to Adam but rather to humankind in common, the authority attendant to property is constrained by the "pressing Wants" of the needy, and again it falls short of political authority.

The Emergence of a Political Narrative

These critical arguments foreshadow the normative concerns with which they are linked in the *Second Treatise*. They clear the ground for subsequent claims about the natural freedom, rationality, and equality of human beings, the consistency of natural freedom with the doctrine of natural law, and the distinction between the authority appropriate to parents, property holders, and magistrates. But precisely because they foreshadow and are thus linked with these familiar positions, they have deflected attention from the more subtle theoretical displacements on which they are predicated. The link with the *Second Treatise* serves to gloss over the remarkable manner in which Locke's polemic with Filmer vitiates a particular manner of writing, arguing, and more generally thinking about politics, and at a more specific level the particular manner of conceptualizing the inclinations, passions, and motives of human beings. I use the term "theoretical displacement" rather than "critique" because, unlike this latter term "displacement" suggests a more fundamentally transformative endeavor in which the parameters and not merely certain specific points of contention are contested and reconceptualized. By focusing on this reconceptualization, I hope to reveal a set of anthropological concerns underlying the more evident and familiar arguments regarding paternal authority and property.

To consider these displacements and set the ground for Locke's reconceptualization, I focus on the manner in which, while critically interpreting Filmer, Locke neutralizes the potential of the Scriptures as the fount of an authoritative political ideal and discourse. In training our attention on the status of Adam's alleged sovereignty, on grounds of either paternity or property, one can lose sight of the degree to which Locke sets a limit, by interjecting a hermeneutic distance, on the very political sovereignty of the Bible and, through it, of God. The importance of such a limit and the role it plays in my larger argument should be emphasized. To manifest the troubling aspects of human beings' cognitive and psychological conditions, Locke must neutralize a way of arguing—namely, scriptural politics—precisely because from within this discourse the gravity of this human condition remains suppressed. He must, in effect, sequester the Bible's status as the source of a credible political anthropology. He does so by restricting the monumentality of the biblical God to that instant when He ushers in creation and thus history. It is from within this history, with all its contingencies and with little residual trace of its divine origins, that the human condition structuring Locke's political thinking emerges. But in making this claim, it is critically important to distinguish it from the claim that Locke is covertly or otherwise denying his faith in biblical precepts. The question of Locke's own faith and even the centrality of this faith for his political thought as evinced, for instance, in his reliance on natural law must be sharply distinguished from the issue of whether this faith serves as the appropriate framework for his political and psychological reflections. The very fact that with Locke such a distinction can be sharply drawn is itself revealing. My purpose and argument turns on the political displacement of scriptural politics and not on denying or impugning Locke's own faith in the Scriptures.

Filmer's paternalist argument is anchored in the precise status of birth, and specifically of Adam's birth. His birth is literally, for Filmer, the inaugural moment of a political and royalist

genealogy that lays down the tracks of a permanent political
settlement. It is therefore a moment invested with a doubly
momentous importance: first, because it marks Adam's own
appointment as monarch; second, because it designates paternalist monarchy as the sole and permanent form of legitimate authority. Consider Locke's construal of this moment:

> Sir Robert in his Preface to his Observations on Aristotle's
> Politicks, tells us, A Natural Freedom of Mankind cannot be
> supposed without the denial of the Creation of Adam [188]:
> but how *Adam's* being Created, which was nothing but his
> receiving a Being immediately from Omnipotency, and the
> hand of God, gave Adam a *Sovereignty* over anything, I cannot
> see . . . for I find no difficulty to suppose the *Freedom of
> Mankind*, though I have always believed in the *Creation of
> Adam;* He was Created, or began to exist, by God's immediate
> Power. . . . And so did the Lion, the King of Beasts before
> him, by the same Creating Power of God: and if bare existence
> by that Power, and in that way, will give Dominion, without
> any more ado, our A—, by this argument, will make the Lion
> have as good a Title to it as he, and certainly the more an-
> cienter. (*First Treatise*, p. 169)

Adam's creation is a moment in time. At best, it is the first
moment in human time. But beyond that it is nothing. It represents the literal and undramatic spectacle of the first incarnation
without any of the resonances the term has traditionally carried.
Intrinsically it has neither moral nor political valency, except a
potentiality associated with being free. In Locke's construal,
neither is Adam created in the image of God nor is his placement
in the Garden of Eden, that emblem of untainted innocence, of
relevance. Creation is the beginning of "bare existence"—an
existence promiscuously repeated in the lion and other creatures.
Indeed, the moment is of such mundane stature that its origin in
the omnipotence of God can be all but overlooked. This is in fact

what Locke's formulation encourages by the synonym he casually offers for Adam's creation: "Adam was Created, or began to exist."

There is no sense in which God's omnipotence carries over to direct or to constrain his creation. Adam is simply released into the world as a receptacle, without a hint of a providential plan— the beginning of history without destiny. Locke has clearly gone beyond his ostensible brief to challenge the doctrine of Adam's sovereignty by birth. Adam's birth, like the lion's, is "nothing but his receiving a Being." It is distinguished simply by being the first of its kind; similarly, Creation is set apart by being the first moment in time. Like Adam, Creation more generally is not marked by the enduring impress of its Creator. On Locke's interpretation, God's omnipotence appears exhausted in the act of Creation. We are told that God could not have appointed Adam to be "Governor of his Posterity" because, at the moment of Creation, Adam had no subjects. Similarly, he could not be a monarch in virtue of fatherhood because, at that point, he had no children. What is striking is that Locke does not even allow God to bestow on Adam any assured potentiality. Adam cannot, therefore, be granted the right of becoming governor as a future assurance nor indeed can he have a similar assurance with respect to his future progeny (p. 172). Locke does not specify whether these divine inabilities stem from a flawed and limited omniscience or from omnipotence. Elsewhere he modifies his view only to the extent that the "strong desire of Self-preservation" is admitted to have its source in divine workmanship (p. 311). Even when Locke speaks of reason as "the Voice of God" in man, he takes this to imply a divine basis for the inclination to preserve one's self and to "increase and multiply," but not as a voice that gives political directives (ibid).

Viewed from the perspective of the Enlightenment, Locke's characterization of Creation can be seen as a momentary point of inflexion before such a characterization became the basis of ei-

ther a rationalist teleological optimism or dismissal of the postu-
late of God in the account of Creation, and therefore as a decisive
moment in the inclination to atheism. In Locke, the thesis of the
natural freedom of human beings, as a thesis pertaining only to
political freedom, still requires God as an efficient—and only
efficient—cause.

It may appear that the point is strained; it may simply confirm, through an exegetical preciosity, what is in any case plainly
evident. To establish the claim of natural freedom, Locke must
divest the discourse of Creation from laying a claim to human
political potentiality. And that indeed is what Locke does. I do
not dispute this claim but only draw out its implications; specifically, I encourage the recognition that what is involved in establishing the thesis of the natural freedom for Locke is to set a limit
on the political sovereignty of God. Accordingly, the style of
theorizing in which such a sovereignty is assumed or projected is
displaced. Underlying this displacement is a concern with a
particular individual the full dimensions of whose troubling
identity could not find expression within scriptural politics. For
the remainder of this chapter, I turn my attention to this individual to reveal how, in Locke's view, its provenance was constrained within scriptural politics and to give a preliminary sense
of the theoretical issues Locke believes attend this emergence.

"Binding Men's Consciences"

The issue through which I consider the problematic of this
individual is that relating to conscience. In the latter part of the
First Treatise, Locke's most persistent assault on Filmer is directed to the latter's inability "to lay obligations to obedience on
any man's conscience." The matter relates to the great question
of all ages, namely, that of "what persons have a right to be
obeyed" (pp. 251–52).

The question of settling human consciences centers Locke's critique of Filmer. Locke invokes it to pressure and expose the limits of scriptural politics along with its claim regarding God's explicit declaration to Adam and by extension his progeny. From the precise mechanics of this pressure, Locke transforms more than he undermines the terms of this dispute. By formulating the question of political obligation via the issue of how human consciences can be settled, and by linking this to the question of the legitimate bearer of political power, Locke consolidates his claim that scripture does not speak to matters of political legitimacy. He does so by both pointing to the already mentioned silence of scripture on these issues and by emphasizing that the issue of political legitimacy is one exclusive to political discourse. Ironically, in the process of this transformation, which is made possible by posing the question of obedience to the dictates of conscience, conscience itself is superseded and replaced by the category of consent. Conscience is all but left out of the *Second Treatise*.

The absence of any discussion of conscience in the *Second Treatise* makes it tempting to view conscience as merely a strategic weapon, one with substantive implications neither relevant nor fully addressed within Locke's own constructive enterprise. Or one might view conscience and consent, as Charles Tarlton does, as "two alternative sources of obligation," with Locke opting for the latter.[18] In contrast, I argue that the question of binding human consciences, far from being a convenient weapon to hurl at Filmer and then discard at will, is in fact central to Locke's own political anxieties, and that its replacement in the *Second Treatise* by consent is at least in part dictated by Locke's inability to settle or assuage its implications. As becomes clearer in the next chapter, conscience resonates in its implications with the imagination as a particularly volatile, inscrutable, and sub-

[18] Tarlton, "A Rope of Sand," p. 62.

jective aspect of human nature. Like the imagination, conscience must ultimately be "settled," disciplined, and rendered transparent. But this, Locke recognizes, is possible only by limiting and directing it in a child's infancy, a theme to which I return in Chapter 4.

In Locke's construal of conscience we glimpse the threatening anthropological potential that is molded in *Thoughts Concerning Education* and controlled through the course of the *Second Treatise*. If this anthropological potential were examined solely in terms of its presence in the *Second Treatise*, one would be liable to mistake it as simply a new and altogether insignificant concept presented in contrast to its theological precursor. At any rate, one would overlook the degree to which the provenance of this cognitive and psychological aspect of modern anthropology is made possible by the mobilizing of new motives under the intensified pressure of older theological concerns.

The great question of government being who has a right to be obeyed, the endurance of government depends on the capacity to bind its citizens' consciences to the continued practice of obeying. This then is the challenge with which Locke confronts Filmer. Filmer must provide sufficient ground to persuade men to bind their consciences. Indeed, Filmer faces a particularly awesome task, since in his view God sanctioned not only one political form but also only one legitimate lineage. The issue for Locke is not whether conscience dictates obedience to God; this is accepted without doubt. Rather, the onus he places on Filmer is to provide a rationale that *will* bind conscience, even though it is the case that "when any such Declaration of God's Intention is produced, it will be our Duty to believe God intends it so" (*First Treatise*, p. 280). Nevertheless,

> it is reasonable to expect, that he [Filmer] should have proved . . . with Arguments clear and evident, suitable to the weightiness of the Cause. That since Men had nothing else left

them, they might in Slavery have such undeniable Proofs of its Necessity, that their Consciences might be convinced, and oblige them to submit peacefully to Absolute Dominion, which their Governors had a Right to exercise over them. Without this, what Good could our A——do, or pretend to do, by erecting such an unlimited Power, but flatter the natural vanity and Ambition of men, too Apt of itself to grow and increase with the Possession of any Power? (P. 166)

To satisfy Locke's challenge, Filmer must prove that God directed us in creating an authority whose scope he defined, placing Adam and his heirs as its executors. But in view of Locke's demand, it is even more important that Filmer establish how the knowledge of God's directives serves to curb the possible deviations from such directives. Already in the formulation of Locke's challenge we can see that his implicit, though central, concern is with restricting possible transgressions of conscience, which in his view appear to be no less likely even if divine precepts are unequivocally established. In the absence of such a demonstration, the most pious among us would be helpless in the face of a truant conscience. It is crucial to recognize that Locke is not asking Filmer to clarify *what* the dictates of conscience are; he is not inquiring into what the Scriptures enjoin us to do and forebear. Rather, his concern is with the evidentiary grounds on which conscience is in fact obliged to obey these dictates.

One can get a sense of Locke's query by considering his focus on the issue of evidence. He systematically accents the need for Filmer to furnish a specific kind of evidence. In the passage just cited we see him pressing for "Arguments clear and evident." In the paragraph that immediately follows, he recalls with incredulity the complete dearth of "that Evidence of Arguments" one would expect Filmer's "main supposition" to be "proved and established with." Filmer's "Fundamental Tenet," we are told, is devoid of "reasons sufficient to justifie the Confidence with which it was assumed." Locke refers with disbelief to the fact "that in a Discourse where he [Filmer] pretends to confute the *Erroneous Principle* of Man's *Natural Freedom*, he should doe it by a bare supposition of *Adam's Authority*, without offering any Proof for that Authority." Finally, with mounting frustration he "finds not one Pretence of a Reason to establish this his great Foundation of Government: not any thing that looks like an Argument" (p. 167).

How are we to interpret this sustained demand for arguments, evidence, and reasons? Is Locke simply interpreting the *Patriarcha*, and in the process discovering that it rests on unjustified premises and that the analytical rigor with which its conclusions are derived is highly questionable? Is he simply exposing an internal incoherence in Filmer's text which limits its theoretical significance? Or rather, is he insinuating an incoherence, and through this maneuver clearing the ground for what I have referred to as a theoretical displacement of scriptural politics? One must then consider what logic Locke finds so conspicuously missing from Filmer's arguments. What would Locke accept as evidence for Adam's alleged grant? And what, in any case, would constitute a reasonable basis for believing or accepting that something other than the severe pedagogical regime Locke proposes and directs at young children in *Thoughts Concerning Education* could bind the consciences of individuals—not to mention individuals who had been forged by the exhilarating transgressiveness of the seventeenth century?

To get a grip on these questions, let us initially consider Locke's perception of Filmer's right to lay claim to the views he expresses. On several occasions Locke questions whether Filmer's credentials are adequate for the views he advances. For a person to propagate divine rule he must, in Locke's words, establish himself "as the Authentick Revealer of God's Intentions" (p. 280). Failing this, Filmer can "not expect that rational and indifferent men should be brought over" (p. 168) to his opinions, "nor can men's Consciences by an other pretence be obliged to it" (ibid.). By driving a wedge between Filmer as author and the opinions expressed in his *Patriarcha*, Locke is not only distancing the author from his text but also clipping the informing authority from the expressed opinions. By casting doubts on the possibility of scriptural precepts having a legitimate and worthy spokesman, Locke is able to confine these precepts beyond our reach and thus avoid questioning their veracity. This is precisely the maneuver by which Hobbes in Part III ("On the Christian Commonwealth") of the *Leviathan* neutralizes the possibility of scripturally guided politics. By implicating the Apostles with his universal conception of human egotism, Hobbes renders suspect their motives and hence their capacity to faithfully transmit the word of Christ.[19] The possibility of a Christian commonwealth is subverted not by questioning the truth of divine precepts but rather by doubting the credibility of those who claim to have had access to these precepts.

But whereas Hobbes, given his view of human motivation, can rightly implicate the Apostles, Locke must simply resort to the skeptical possibility that Filmer's arguments for absolute monarchy are spurred by "some other . . . interest" (p. 168). Locke's suggestion that Filmer is not an authentic revealer of God's intentions is no more compelling to Filmer than would be Locke's thorough denial of Filmer's faith. To ask of Filmer to

[19] In Hobbes's words, "When God speaketh to man, it must be either immediately; or by mediation of another man, to whom he had formerly spoken by himself immediately. How God speaketh to a man immediately may be understood by those well enough, to whom he hath so spoken; but how the same should be understood by another, is hard, if not impossible to know"; *Leviathan* , p. 410. This passage summarizes the conceptual thrust on account of which Hobbes confines and relegates scriptural authority; see J. G. A. Pocock, "Time, History and Eschatology in the Thought of Thomas Hobbes," in *Politics, Language and Time* (New York: Atheneum, 1973), pp. 163–65. Descartes in Rule III of the *Regulae* points out that there is no way to make spontaneous contact with what others say or think; also see Rule XII, *quidquid ex aliis audimus.*

validate his faith is to ask him to do that which his faith allows him to ignore. It was common knowledge that the precepts of revelation are not accessible to reason or available to the discursive practice that infers consequences from given premises. Moreover, they are inaccessible to experience, since their content does not refer to phenomena that could thereby be sensed and remembered. Similarly, for Locke to demand a more authentic source of God's intentions than that found in the Holy Writ is for him to introduce an adventitious distinction, which Filmer as believer can and does ignore. Locke's contention that Filmer cannot consistently author his own views regarding divine rule can be sustained only by sharply distinguishing between God's intentions and the embodiment of these intentions in the Scriptures. For Filmer, the latter embodies the former; hence they hardly need be distinguished.

The purpose of this digression into Locke's view of Filmer's authority as an author is to highlight a strategic move that is common to Locke's demand for arguments, reasons, and evidence. When Locke announces that "it is reasonable to expect, that [Filmer] should have proved . . . with arguments clear and evident" the grounds whereby "Consciences might be convinced," he is using the term "reasonable" with deceptive specificity (p. 166). Filmer does not share Locke's conception of what is clear and evident. For the former, nothing is more profoundly obliging, nothing more obviously reasonable and evident, than scriptural precepts. Laslett quite rightly emphasizes, in his introduction to the *Patriarcha*, that Filmer's "prime assumption was that the Bible was the true, the unique and complete revelation of God's will on all things."[20] Where Locke with rhetorical amazement finds Adam's sovereignty "taken for granted without proof" (p. 167), Filmer would, with equally assured conviction,

---

[20] Peter Laslett, "Introduction" to Sir Robert Filmer, *Patriarcha*, in *Patriarcha and Other Political Works*, ed. Peter Laslett (Oxford: Basil Blackwell, 1949), p. 11.

deny the need for any such proof. Filmer explicitly states that he will "have nothing to do" with those who compromise with that "erroneous principle of man's Natural Freedom." The monarchic edifice of Filmer's scriptural politics rests firmly only if faith is unquestioningly presupposed.[21] The literary confrontation that suggests a dialogical acceptance of first premises conceals the radically divergent starting points of Locke and Filmer. It is not that Locke denies the veracity of scripture; rather, he denies it as evidence for the foundation of government. Locke's demand for "Arguments" instead of Filmer's "suppositions without Proof" transforms, despite rhetorical concealment, the terms of the discourse.

Locke's calls for evidence, reasons, and arguments serve as textual fences whereby he brackets and displaces Filmer's substantive claims and concerns. By rendering the object of Filmer's faith hermeneutically inaccessible, that is, literally speechless, the constitution of a new object of theory is made possible. In contrast with the predestination involved in Filmer's theological monarchism, and the corresponding indifference with which it views human needs and capacities and specifically cognitive capacities, there is emerging in Locke's textual maneuvers a theory that both accents human cognitive power and is threatened by this very plenitude. Instead of the repose of theoretical quietude in which salvation is tied to an unfathomable divine decree, Locke's theory presumes a self-assertive and aggressive cognitive endowment in which such postures cannot be left inscrutable. Here we may anticipate the eagerness with which Locke in the very first chapter of the *Second Treatise* emphasizes the "Right of *making* Laws" (p. 286, emphasis added) in his definition of political power.

Locke's demand for reasons, arguments, and evidence is simultaneously a challenge and the announcement of a new theoretical and political program. Jean Gerson's famous fifteenth-

[21] *Patriarcha*, p. 54.

century dictum *Credite evangelio et sufficit* (Believe in the Gospel and it is enough) expresses a theoretical self-restriction that can now no longer be sustained. In its stead a new theoretical curiosity is emerging, championed under the banner of reason which will root itself by emphasizing the human care (*cura*) it brings with it.[22]

Filmer's concerns are ossified. Perhaps like all reactionary thought they strike the world at a tangent. Their aesthetic and theological coherence belies their political irrelevance. By their trans-historical fixity they cannot be rejuvenated. And once a new set of motives have emerged, they can be understood only by being distorted. Of the former sentiment one gets a powerful sense from Locke's frustration with Filmer's language. The "Intricacy of [Filmer's] Words" have a "Doubtfullness of . . . Meaning." His "doubtful and general terms makes such a medley and confusion that it is impossible to show his Mistakes" (pp. 173–74). Even in its errors, Filmer's language retains a coherent indifference to the world, or rather, the world now displays an indifference to his errors. All that remains is the outer mantle of language, insignificant words defiantly pegged to implausible convictions. As Locke puts it, "By such a use of Words, one may say any thing." In contrast, Locke will "speak less learnedly, and more Intelligibly" (pp. 172–73). Filmer's language is too stiff to intelligibly capture the concerns that have overtaken it. One gets the sense of a tired system of thought, tottering under the weight of its own senseless erudition.[23]

It would, however, be a mistake to think of Filmer's thought as

---

[22] Blumenberg, *Legitimacy of the Modern Age*, pp. 329–436.

[23] Hobbes conveys a similar impression with regard to the language of "Schoole-Divines," which is "for the most part, but insignificant Traines of strange and barbarous words, or words otherwise used, than in the common use of the Latine tongue"; *Leviathan*, pp. 701–2. As with Locke, Hobbes is concerned with the extent to which the language of the Schools has lost touch with common usages. In the "Review and Conclusion," Hobbes presents this idea graphicly, as an "argument of Indigestion, when Greek and Latine Sentences *unchewed* come up again, as they use to do, *unchanged*"; *Leviathan*, p. 727.

simply theological deadweight ineluctably approaching a historical precipice. It would also be unfair to the intellectual labors of
the *First Treatise* to view them merely as attempts to expedite
Filmer's precipitous fall. To give credence to this spatial image of
theoretical displacement, one must have a clear sense of the
theoretical engagement that precedes it. In any case, ideas like
institutions, however outdated, often show a remarkable capacity to balance on the knife edge between artifice and unreality. In
this they are often aided by what Peter Brown calls "the unbounded capacity of human beings for irrelevance."[24] To think
of Filmer as an instrumentally convenient strawman would be
only to confirm the attitude that has resulted in a corresponding
indifference toward the *First Treatise*. It is true that Locke does
use the *Patriarcha* to insinuate his own concerns. This itself,
however presumes a theoretical purpose for which the *Patriarcha*
must have been perceived as useful. Moreover, what is perceived
as useful may be so precisely because it makes itself available as a
counterpoint for the entry of a variant discourse. Locke's discussion of the binding of human conscience is, I think, an instance
of such a theoretical move.

I have already indicated that for Locke the curbing of conscience is linked by its association to obedience to the "great
questions" of how to settle governments. If considered with all
its perceived ramifications, it is perhaps the single most important objection Locke raises in the *First Treatise*.[25] Stated briefly,
Locke's claim is that if Filmer cannot "teach obedience," if he
cannot satisfy human consciences of the "Fatherhood of Adam"
(p. 259), then he cannot rightfully expect the obedience necessary for the establishment of a government. Let us consider the
political relevance of this question from Filmer's perspective. In

[24] Peter Brown, *Society and the Holy in Late Antiquity* (Berkeley: University of
California Press, 1982), p. 29.
[25] Tarlton, in "A Rope of Sand," convincingly brings out this significance; see
especially pp. 60–65.

what manner, if at all, is the settling of government for Filmer predicated on the curbing of human consciences?

Nowhere in the *Patriarcha*, in fact in none of what Laslett refers to as Filmer's political works, is conscience mentioned. Filmer simply does not use the term. And with good reason: it refers to a concern quite alien to him, and of its threatening implications Filmer is blissfully oblivious. Nor does obedience present Filmer with the problem that it does for Locke. In Filmer's revealingly brief tract on obedience he finds the issue settled in favor of his patriarchal views by the unanimously accepted view regarding the "original subjection in children, to be governed by their parents." Any notion of "an original freedom" is therefore palpably contradictory.[26] Later in the same work, he repeats his claim with redoubled conviction: "Every man that is born, is so far from being free-born, that by his very birth he becomes a subject to him that begets him: under which subjection he is always to live, unless by immediate appointment from god, or by the grant or death of his Father, he become possessed of that power to which he was subject."[27] Given such self-certain assurance of our original and eternal servitude in view of God's scriptural grant to Adam, Filmer rightly finds the question of obedience settled from its very source. It is not the binding of our conscience but rather the intensification of our faith which guides Filmer's work. And it is in the latter that the settling of government finds its source, authority, and destiny.

All this might be taken to suggest that Locke's challenge and rebuke of Filmer is unfair, and if not that at least somewhat devious. Locke, it might be said, conceals Filmer's radically different purposes and the presuppositions that give them their coherence, only to give the appearance of a fair encounter when in fact it is a staged dispute. This may, in part be true, for the

---

[26] Sir Robert Filmer, "Direction for Obedience to Government," in *Patriarcha*, pp. 331–35.

[27] Ibid., p. 333. This view is repeated constantly in the *Patriarcha*.

reader of the *First Treatise* is certainly led to believe that the rationale for the binding of conscience is a textually relevant demand Filmer simply ignores. But if one is to speak of interpretative duplicity on Locke's part, one must consider the motives and the larger project underlying his affectations. Why does Locke pressure Filmer's text with the question of binding human conscience? What, for Locke, is the theoretical and concrete purchase of substituting Filmer's concern with the intensification of faith by the question of restricting the possibilities of the individual conscience? What, in short, are the pressing issues Locke associates with the question of conscience?

The theme of conscience runs through all Locke's political and moral works. From his early writings (*Essays on the Law of Nature*, 1660; *Two Tracts of Government*, 1660) to his mature works (*Essay Concerning Human Understanding*, 1690; *A Letter on Toleration*, 1689; *Two Treatises of Government*, 1689) one finds an unmistakable engagement and consistency in his views on conscience. Consider these, for instance:

> Indeed, all obligation binds conscience, and lays a bond on the mind itself, so that not fear of punishment, but a rational apprehension of what is right, puts us under an obligation, and conscience passes judgment on morals, and if we are guilty of a crime, declares that we deserve punishment.[28]

> Imposing on conscience seems to me to be the pressing of doctrines or laws upon the belief or practice of men as of the divine original, . . . when indeed they are no other but the ordinances of men and the products of their authority.[29]

The law of conscience we call that fundamental judgment of

[28] John Locke, *Essays on the Law of Nature*, ed. W. von Leyden (Oxford: Clarendon Press, 1958), p. 135.

[29] John Locke, *Two Tracts on Government*, ed. Philip Abrams (Cambridge: Cambridge University Press, 1967), p. 148.

the practical intellect concerning any possible truth of a moral proposition about things to be done in life.[30]

Moral actions belong therefore to the jurisdiction of both the outward and the inward court, and are subject to both dominions, of the civil as well as the domestic governor: I mean both of the magistrate and of conscience.[31]

Conscience . . . is nothing else but our own Opinion or Judgement of the Moral Rectitude or pravity of our own actions. (*Essay*, p. 70)

To settle Government in the World, and lay Obligations to obedience on any man's Conscience, it is necessary . . . to satisfie him, who has a Right to this Power. (*First Treatise*, p. 248)

It is clear from these brief extracts that Locke's view of conscience undergoes some development. Nevertheless, it is fair to say that there is an enduring sense in which conscience refers, for Locke, to the aspect of moral judgments in which individuals are alone and which they reserve for themselves. Related to this, though more important, the legal metaphor by which conscience is viewed as an inner court points to an even deeper realm where the need for proscribing and prescribing the content of conscience is deemed necessary. Consider for instance the language and sentiment (in both respects strikingly Kantian) of the following extract from the *Two Tracts:* "There should be an inner legislator [in effect] constantly present in us whose edicts it should not be lawful for us to transgress even nails breadth."[32] The imperative to confine possible transgression is similarly echoed in the suggestion from the early *Essays* in which Locke

---

[30] Ibid., p. 225.

[31] John Locke, *A Letter on Toleration* (Indianapolis: Bobbs-Merrill, 1980), p. 46.

[32] Locke, *Two Tracts*, p. 225.

speaks of the need to police and punish improper moral judgments and actions. In his later works and especially in *Some Thoughts Concerning Education;* the theme of disciplining the realm of interiority and the political ramification he associates with such disciplining become unmistakably major concerns.

I am suggesting that Locke's obsession with the curbing of conscience, a concern totally absent in Filmer's work, is indicative of a deeper philosophical unease about the instability and threatening volatility with which Locke regards the realm of subjective cognitive experience. The need for self-legislating circumscription and corresponding punition with which Locke identifies the deepest core of human judgment—conscience—reveals an equally deep anxiety with respect to what is now deemed possible if this core is left unbounded. In contrast, by viewing the individual, both politically and morally, as being thoroughly directed by faith, and in thinking of such a faith as the basis of a permanent political settlement, Filmer obviates the entire question of curbing conscience. Where Filmer leaves as unproblematic the question of obedience by linking it to the simple intensity of faith, Locke fractures Filmer's text by burdening it with a novel set of psychological and cognitive considerations. The question of obedience is thus the fixed point that allows the introduction of new concerns through the substitution of faith by conscience, but in this substitution is inscribed a project that has its fullest expression in Locke's discussion of the human capacity to imagine and fantasize.

The obviously different political preferences of Filmer and Locke conceal subtle though profound differences in the individual for which each is writing. By presuming an internal subjective coherence that no longer exists, Filmer's conservative doctrine is forced into a reactionary posture. The stable order within which he assumes a permanent and intuitive obligatory bond to scriptural precepts is made more rigid the moment this ethic has to be supported by arguments with reasoned evidence. The coherence of Filmer's views resides in their being taken for granted. When Filmer's spiritual system of providence—the cornerstone of his patriarchal politics—began to be questioned, it also ceased to be credible. Locke's surgical scrutiny of Filmer's beliefs does not so much disturb their coherence as render them irrelevant. John Dunn is quite right to say that "the entire *First Treatise*, which is designed to discredit Filmer's extrapolations from the Old Testament, ends up making the latter seem almost irrelevant to issues of political right."[33] But whereas Dunn seems to find this surprising, I suggest, in contrast, that the move that renders Filmer irrelevant is made from a position that allows Locke to introduce a radically different set of concerns. When, speaking of Filmer's use of Scripture to establish the right of fathers to rule toward the end of the *First Treatise*, Locke says "records are utterly silent" (p. 265), he must, in large measure, be understood to have effected this silence.

In contrast with Filmer's, Locke's individuals are "naturally" free. This does not by itself mean that they are *not* pious or faithful Christians. Nor does this necessitate a denial of scripture as a legitimate basis of political right and power. Still less does the assumption of natural freedom mean that it will be used or misused to transgress the bounds of human civility or any given set of political or moral norms. Although none of these are necessary, the fact of natural freedom makes all of them possible; and this despite the fact that for Locke natural freedom refers to the circumscribed realm of political choices. These possibilities, however remote they may have appeared, bring into the political and theoretical domain a variety of new concerns. If, as Locke believes, a political treatise must accept as its historical starting point an individual with a "Natural Vanity and Ambition . . . [that is] Apt *of it self* to grow and increase" (p. 166, emphasis added), then the question of obedience cannot, *pace* Filmer, be

---

[33] Dunn, *Political Thought of John Locke*, p. 99.

left to a presumed and preferred intensity of religious faith. Similarly, if the human "natural" quest of power is *"of it self . . . too keen"* (p. 257, emphasis added), then the question of who is to govern cannot be left to the doubtful vagaries of finding Adam's rightful heir. If, moreover, the surest testament of our being free is the fact of our being human, then the political subjection of Eve and the female gender cannot be assumed as part of "the Original Grant of Government" (p. 190). Nor, if God gave all human beings an "intellectual" Nature (p. 197), can physical weakness be made the basis of conflating "Conjugal Power" and "Political Power" (p. 190).

It is, one might say, on behalf of these distinctly modern individuals—modern not simply because they are free but, more important, because in the externalizing of their natures they extend the horizons of their freedom—that Locke pitches his attack against Filmer. Conscience, as the deepest core of this nature, exemplifies for Locke the existential program within which the extension of boundaries is, as it were, naturally immanent. Especially if one acknowledges its link with the imagination, conscience leads, in Locke's view, of itself to dangerously extreme and extravagant pursuits, and this precisely because it derives its energy from an inscrutable and autonomous source of human motivation. It is this self-assertive energy that cannot, without totally surrendering itself, accept Filmer's ordered world apprehended by faith. Similarly, it cannot admit the providential view that the armature of politics lies in a distant past beyond human reach. The possibility held out to humanity of escaping into transcendence, simply by grasping the absolutism of divine decree, has lost its relevance because this absolutism involves an unacceptable dependence of human salvation. When Locke, at the outset of the *First Treatise*, announces, "I . . . cannot but think [myself] a Freeman" (p. 176), one must not overlook the sheer facticity with which he presents this self-definition. Similarly, in formulations such as "I leave the Reader to Judge; and to believe if he can, that these words of *Isaac, be Lord over thy Brethren, and let thy Mothers Sons bow down to thee,* confirm'd *Jacob in a Sovereignty over Esau,* upon the account of the Birthright he had got from him" (p. 265) we must recognize the extent to which Locke finds Filmer's views simply contrary to what is now possible. Human interests and cogitations cannot, as with Filmer, be positioned beyond the domain of human self-assertion.

From Locke's handling of conscience, I have tried to intimate a sense of the questions which, in his view, are linked to the political project of individualism and husbanded through the course of the *Two Treatises.* As I mentioned earlier, it is Locke's recognition of the unpredictability and extravagance of human motivation that makes the subjectivity implicit in conscience paradigmatic of his larger political anxieties. This is not to suggest that Locke can sustain the view of conscience as being part of the political realm. Indeed, judging by its almost total exclusion from the *Second Treatise* and the radical sequestering of the "magistrates court" from the "inner court" in the *Letter Concerning Toleration,* Locke appears to place it outside the putatively political domain. This displacement of conscience is, I think, itself an attempt to circumscribe the politically significant potentialities of human subjectivity. But it is this very need to fortify the political domain from subjective fancies that makes the problem of political obedience analogous to the problem of binding human conscience and, as the next chapter suggests, to the nest of problems associated with the imagination.

CHAPTER THREE

Curiosity, Imagination, and Madness

The difference betwixt a madman and one in his wits consisted in this: that the former spoke out whatever came into his mind, and just in the confused manner as his *imagination* presented the ideas. The latter only expressed such thoughts as his judgment directed him to chuse, leaving the rest to die away in his memory. And that if the wisest man would at any time utter his thoughts, in the crude indigested manner as they came into his head, he would be looked upon as raving mad.

—Jonathan Swift

Liberalism seems fated to be burdened with a plurality of meanings. Notwithstanding the precise and well-defined way in which the term is used by some scholars, in common parlance it triggers an enormous range of associations and resonances. In this variety and flexibility of connotations, even if in little else, the contemporary usage of the term recapitulates an aspect common to its historical provenance. Interpretations of the historical situation from which liberalism emerged and to which it was a response are famously various. The religious wars of the late sixteenth and seventeenth centuries, the denominational conflicts in the aftermath of the Reformation, the logical extension of Puritan individualism, the settlement of church and crown relations, the political and economic creed of emerging capitalism, the ideological gloss requisite for incipient European imperialism, not to mention more specific events such as the English civil war or "the Popish problem," have all, with varying degrees of credibility, been proffered as the wellspring from which liberalism arose. Each such interpretation not only gives a distinct explanatory account but also in the process features and emphasizes distinct aspects of the textual corpus of liberalism.

Despite the variety of these accounts and the distinct problematic associated with the various historical situations they draw on, if one approaches liberalism from a textual study of Hobbes's and Locke's works, one confronts, relatively speaking, a fairly precise and widely agreed on nest of motivating problems. At the broadest level, within this textual perspective, individuals are viewed as naturally free, rational, and equal and are assumed to have an interest in their preservation, their liberty, and their property. The pursuit of these interests in the absence of a superintending authority leads to the prospect of a dire situation that both Hobbes and Locke characterize as a state of war. Liberal political institutions profess to avert this prospect by articulating the basis for such a superintending authority and justifying the constraints it imposes on human freedom and, in the case of Locke, on natural rights by reference to the rationally accessible interest of each individual which such authority would secure.

This, in brief, is the narrative on the basis of which Hobbes's and Locke's political projects are most commonly understood, endorsed, modified, and criticized. It appeals to an abstract conception of the constitutive features of human nature. It demonstrates by reference to the appetitive and self-interested aspects of this nature and certain broad circumstances of human interaction the consequences immanent in their unregulated interactions. Finally, it aims to justify both the means and the extent of the regulative redress—that is, political authority—by showing it to be, at least counterfactually, in the interest of each individual and hence the basis on which a unanimous contractual agreement could be reached to create such authority. With

Locke, the implications of these foundational assumptions are said to lead to a defense of constitutional government whose power is held in trust from the people who remain sovereign. This power is further limited by the right the people retain to judge whether the government is fulfilling the terms of the trust, exercising it through the appropriate juridical means and employing it to serve their common interests.

The Naturalistic Problematic: Interests and Appetites

The account outlined above is familiar, and attendant to it are a familiar set of critical questions that have served as the mainstay of much of Locke scholarship. If, for instance, the institutional arrangements endorsed by Locke are said to derive from his foundational assumptions regarding human freedom, equality, and rationality, then it is to be expected that scholars would ask whether such a derivation is in fact consistent and exhaustive. Alternatively, are there perhaps other assumptions which, as Leo Strauss suggested, surreptitiously inform and structure Locke's work and furthermore impugn his benign surface conclusions? Or, as C. B. Macpherson claimed, are these conclusions in any case only coherent on account of some historically assumed but textually obscured set of economic and sociological biases? Do Locke's institutions in fact possess the requisite resources to satisfy the task of securing peace and order, or are they, as Hobbes would suggest, by virtue of their internal plurality and the limits placed on them doomed to disintegrate and thus perpetuate the "inconveniences" of the state of nature? Alternatively, do Locke's foundational commitments place real limits on legitimate political authority or are these in fact overridden by, for instance, his concessions to executive prerogative? As a corollary, are the rights of individuals in fact secure against the authority Locke grants the state? More recently, it has been asked whether Locke's abstract views of human nature are consistent with the legitimacy he ascribes to a formally restricted property owner's state. Feminist scholars have considered the question of the precise status of women's political rights, and, given Locke's famously illusive discussion of this issue, the perspective from which this question should be considered.[1] These questions are themselves part of a more general query into the terms of a normative association that free, equal, and rational individuals would agree to.

As a rough characterization of the lines along which recent Locke scholarship has interrogated his political texts, this list is not exhaustive. For this, no apology need be made, for such a task would in any case be close to impossible. Rather, the list is offered to help frame an alternative reading without, of course, denying the links between this alternative and the more canonical approach.

It is, I think, a striking feature of much of recent Locke scholarship that it accepts the characterization of the individual in terms of freedom, equality, and rationality as foundational. This is meant to indicate that these attributes literally serve as the foundation or base on which it is assumed subsequent claims rely. The stability and coherence of these notions is thus taken for granted. To be more precise, the individual conceived in terms of natural freedom, rationality, and equality is taken to be a sufficiently stable and coherent conceptualization and who, for that very reason, can serve as the foundational base from which to consider the normative question of what institutions comport with the interests and natural rights of such an individual. This is not to suggest that notions such as freedom, rationality, and

---

[1] Carol Pateman's discussion in *The Sexual Contract* (Stanford: Stanford University Press, 1988), is, I believe, the most sustained and engaging consideration of this particular line of thought.

equality are not elaborated, or that these elaborations, especially regarding rationality, do not assume considerable complexity and subtlety. Rather, it is to point to a persistent and widespread deference in which the psychological and cognitive drives underpinning these notions are seldom uncovered or their implications acknowledged as bearing on the structures and institutions of political society. It is as though the characterization of these attributes as natural has enclosed them within a hardened shelter imbued with a presumptive coherence. There is in this what one might call a persistent Aristotelianism, for Aristotle essential human nature is justified simply by being realized and hence requires no further elaboration with respect to other existential purposes. As an instance of this nature, human cognitive drive is assessed simply by virtue of one's relation to the perceptual world and the delight one takes in access to it through the senses.[2] Locke himself has been accused of a psychological naivete that is said to impugn the foundations of his own political conclusions.[3]

Putting aside the question of whether such deference or indifference has its roots in Locke or in subsequent perspectives, one can still point to the effects of this perspective on the paths we follow and the puzzles we construct and pursue. By ignoring the psychological and cognitively febrile traces in the Lockean individual for whom notions of freedom, equality, and rationality are fraught and intermixed, in Locke's view, with anxieties regarding an absence of self-control, an extravagance of imaginative fantasy that can masquerade as reason, and more generally a hyperactive set of passions, we sidestep the wider and enormously rich terrain of what James Tully has recently and very aptly called the

[2] Aristotle, *Metaphysics*, 1.1.980a21. Also see Blumenberg, *Legitimacy of the Modern Age*, pp. 243–62.

[3] See Laski, *Political Thought in England*, p. 24: "Few great thinkers have so little perceived the psychological foundations of politics."

"governing of conduct."[4] In brief, we overlook the processes and the myriad of institutions—familial, educational, economic, religious, and hence only partially political—through which the individual hopefully *comes to be* free, rational, and equal in the appropriate manner. In ignoring, or at any rate deemphasizing, the range and significance of these various interdictions and pressures through which the modern individual is constituted, we obscure our view of that vast constellation of interlinked associations that both historically and currently comes under the umbrella of liberalism. More important, by not acknowledging these associations and the role they play, and by considering instead the liberal problematic in narrowly political terms, we are liable to fail to see the often contradictory inducements and pressures pulling on the modern liberal citizen. Finally and most important, we risk overlooking and hence misunderstanding the vast array of institutions or, to use Foucault's term, technologies through which the individual—not the natural individual with reason and interests, but the individual with strange passions, with a frenzied imagination, with undisciplined and chaotic urges—is molded and transformed to have particular passions, an ordered imagination, controlled and well-occasioned urges; in brief, to be rational and self-interested and as a result perhaps also strangely confined. It is these and similar omissions that underlie and sustain the hubris of platitudes such as that liberalism considers all individuals as naturally free, rational, and equal.

It is worth briefly elaborating the theoretical presumptions that lead one to overlook the problematic on which this work focuses. Ironically, this failure is, I believe, linked to a narrow overvaluation of Locke as a political theorist. By this I mean that

---

[4] Tully, "Governing Conduct." This excellent article not only synthesizes an enormous mass of material but also sets out the broad contours for interesting further research.

the central problem in need of theoretical elaboration is taken to be a concern with the basis, justification, and nature of political authority. Locke's problem is conceived in terms of theoretically artificing a primus inter pares that is to serve as a bridge for the transition from the state of nature to the commonwealth. He is, on this reckoning, concerned exclusively with a political question, and the reason for this narrow focus is easy to understand.

Locke's state of nature—as so many commentators have pointed out, especially in contrast to the corresponding state in Hobbes—is visibly blessed by the elaborate integuments of social order. Life within it is structured and supported by family relations, property relations, contractual relations that include the buying and selling of commodities such as labor and goods, and a monetized economy that encompasses riches at home and abroad. Corresponding to these various relations are the norms of authority Locke believes appropriate to them: fathers have power over their children and wives, masters over their servants, and lords over their slaves (*Second Treatise*, p. 286). Underpinning this complex social organization are individuals who are assumed to have reason and are thus, at least potentially, capable of understanding, interpreting, and hence willfully living within the restrictions of the laws of nature that give this state its ethical moorings. They are also, for that reason, competent with respect to the natural rights that allow them juridical freedom and the executive power to punish violations of those laws. Indeed, one might think that individuals in Locke's state of nature manifest as an aspect of their natural endowment that most elevated of Enlightenment ethical norms, "where there is no Law, there is no Freedom" (*Second Treatise*, p. 324). And, as would be expected of such individuals, they evince a developed set of sentiments such as love, charity, and sympathy. It is, in brief, a state that has none of the agonizing social and anarchic impoverishment Hobbes associates with the natural condition:

In such [a] condition, there is no place for industry; because the fruit thereof is uncertain: and consequently no culture of the earth; no navigation, nor use of the commodities that may be imported by sea; no commodious building; no instruments of moving, and removing, such things as require much force; no knowledge of the face of the earth; no account of time; no arts; no letters; no society; and which is worst of all, continual fear, and danger of violent death.[5]

By starting from a thoroughly evacuated foundation, Hobbes is committed to justify an authority with the expansive power sufficient to construct and regulate virtually every detail of it.[6] In this he is reminiscent, despite other obvious and important differences, of Plato's polis, which has a virtual monopoly of power. It alone is the source, the executor, and the arbiter of judgments. It structures the family and the major social institutions of society; it orders the polity by reference to standards that are largely indifferent to the subjective perceptions and preferences of individuals.

The contrast with Hobbesian and ancient absolutism appears to corroborate the common view of Locke as one who avoids these excesses by eschewing the need to fashion order ab initio; instead, by recognizing the settled assurances of the natural condition, he limits himself to the specific problem of political order. This self-limitation and the assurances on which it is based are the background to another familiar restriction in which

---

[5] Thomas Hobbes, *Leviathan*, chap. 13.

[6] The *Leviathan* opens with the methodological justification for precisely this expansive constructive project. The first few lines of the introduction are devoted to "artifice," or construction: "Nature (the Art whereby God hath made and governes the World) is by the *Art* of man, as in many other things, so in this also imitated, that it can make an Artificial Animal. . . . *Art* goes yet further, imitating that Rationall and most excellent worke of Nature, *Man*"; *Leviathan*, p. 81.

the justified power of the state is itself limited. After all, in the presence of such natural conveniences and abundance, one might understandably be led to query the need for legitimizing anything more than highly circumscribed political authority. Indeed, when toward the end of the *Second Treatise* Locke reconsiders the question "why will he give up this Empire [i.e., the state of nature], and subject himself to the Dominion and Control of any other Power," his response, especially if placed alongside the deadly stakes attached to the corresponding transition in Hobbes, seems singularly undramatic. It is simply the uncertainty of enjoying one's property in the face of the appetitive pursuits of others (p. 368). Even if to this is added Locke's previously mentioned reference to the tendency of people to be partial to themselves in interpreting the laws of nature, the combined effect of these two reasons seems scarcely commensurate with the enormity of the changes in the natural condition they occasion. It is not surprising that some liberals, including on occasion Locke himself, have always been tempted with the fantasy of all but banishing political institutions and leaving things to the blissful and self-regulating workings of the natural order.[7] Where the bonds and enormous complexity of society are deemed to be natural, it is perhaps to be expected that such an endowment would provoke the naive presumption that all the problems of peace, order, and social conduct might have a similar redress.

This is the problematic to which Locke is assumed to be responding. It has its textual basis in a perfectly plausible, even if rather narrow, reading of the first few chapters of the *Second Treatise*. It has also become a kind of archetype for much subse-

---

[7] Consider the comment Locke makes, again toward the end of the *Second Treatise:* "And were it not for the corruption, and viciousness of degenerate Men, there would be no need of any other; no necessity that Men should separate from this great and natural Community, and by positive agreements combine into smaller and divided associations" (p. 370).

quent liberal theorizing. Moreover, in America at least, it has reigned as the paradigmatic code of popular political discourse that takes freedom and equality as self-evident truths and views the state with the admixture of self-assured contempt, pride, and awe that might be reserved for a sovereign or leviathan.

The foundational assumptions of human freedom, rationality, and equality which for Locke were the heuristic basis for prying loose the stifling associations of class, guild, gender, church, and state—the terms in which medieval and early modern society defined and confined individuals—have become in effect the grounds for a perspective that overlooks Locke's own modifications and reformulations of these social designations. Here an insight from Louis Hartz's famous work on American liberalism is helpful both to explain partially this oversight and to supply at least some of its major contextual contours. As is well known, Hartz identified the absence of feudalism as the distinctive historical feature that allowed one to read Locke in America without having to acknowledge the revolutionary social impact with which he was linked by historical contiguity in Europe: "When Locke came to America because the basic feudal oppression of Europe had not taken root, the fundamental social norm of Locke ceased in large part to look like a norm and began, of all things, to look like a sober description of fact."[8] This insight in a strange way applies to interpretations that have accepted the naturalism of Locke's foundational assumptions about freedom, rationality, and equality as though they were sober descriptions of anthropological fact without recognizing the enormous richness of detailed design and craft that lie, as it were, behind such appearances. To restate the point, it is as though that ambiguous privilege Tocqueville identified as distinctive to America of being "born free" rather than of having to become so has become,

---

[8] Louis Hartz, *The Liberal Tradition in America* (New York: Harcourt Brace, 1955), p. 60.

through an ironic transposing of text and context, a standard for the perspective we impose on Locke's work.

The implications of overemphasizing the naturalism of Locke's foundational assumptions, and in fact of considering these assumptions as foundational in a narrow sense, are considerable and far reaching. As a general matter, such an approach overstates Locke's preoccupation with a narrowly conceived political problem—that of justifying political authority along with all the familiar limits placed on it. The question of the precise manner in which Locke was concerned with limiting political authority is by the nature of the issue an important one. But for that reason it must not be assessed by exclusive reference to the alleged limits he places on political institutions alone. The issue of placing limits on political power is tied not only to the manner in which individuals interact with each other but also to the habits, the practices, and the rules within which their subjectivity is expressed.

This observation suggests a more specific implication of what I have called the overvaluation of Locke's political problematic. By viewing the need for political society as originating simply in people's conflictual interests and natural partiality toward themselves, one minimizes Locke's own recognition of a range of issues that bear on the need for and origins of political society.

Both self-interest and partiality are taken to be natural features of the self; their form and object may vary but, barring that, they have an almost biological status.[9] They are, as such, beyond the reach of intervention and modification. Thus, they have been the preferred grounds on which to explain human behavior because their identification suggests a causal motive that trumps the unwieldy gloss of categories such as culture, social class, values, intentions, and other subjective explanations. By inter-

[9] See Jane Mansbridge, ed., *Beyond Self-Interest* (Chicago: University of Chicago Press, 1990).

preting political society as consequent to them alone, one gives such interpretations an apparent theoretical robustness and the institutions of such a society a general applicability. As a general matter, this emphasis slights the importance of cognitive considerations. There is an irony here, because Locke himself viewed such cognitive features as natural, at any rate no less natural than the urging of the appetites. So one can imagine a quite distinct historiography of Locke scholarship and of liberal scholarship more generally in which cognitive features would have had far greater salience and in which the appetites and interests would not have defined the norm. But that is another story, aspects of which are evident in the development of the English novel during the eighteenth century. It is not at all surprising that Locke's status in this tradition to which he did not directly contribute is nevertheless that of a prodigiously influential godfather.[10]

There are several reasons for resisting this all but canonical approach to the study of Locke and liberalism. In the study of human motivation, it is now widely accepted that self-interest neither exhausts the range of human motivations nor accurately models the actual motives underlying human activity. From a normative perspective, it is similarly far from clear that the institutions we should design are those that can be supported by people acting on self-interested grounds. Nor is it the case that the institutions of Western democracy are in fact exclusively supported by such motives and behavior.[11] In the present context,

[10] Patricia Meyer Spacks, *Imagining a Self: Autobiography and Novel in Eighteenth Century England* (Cambridge: Harvard University Press, 1976). Also see Ernest Tuveson, *The Imagination as a Means of Grace: Locke and the Aesthetics of Romanticism* (Berkeley: University of California Press, 1960); Douglas Patey, *Probability and Literary Form: Philosophic Theory and Literary Practice in the Augustan Age* (Cambridge: Cambridge University Press, 1984).

[11] All these claims are amply supported and elaborated in *Beyond Self-Interest*, the distinguished collection of essays edited by Jane Mansbridge. See, in particular, Mansbridge's introduction and the essays by A. K. Sen, Jon Elster, and Tom Tyler.

my reason for resisting this naturalistic approach is that it fails to appreciate a central source of Locke's own concerns regarding the individual and the basis and preconditions of political society. It fails, that is, as an adequate key to an understanding of Locke's texts. This failure can be summarized as a failure to appreciate the extent to which Locke is troubled by the natural capacities of the mind and, as a specific instance of this, its capacity and tendency to be governed by an overexcited imagination. In underappreciating this dimension, the naturalistic and appetitive focus ultimately fails in its understanding of the broader historical and intellectual context of seventeenth- and eighteenth-century political, psychological, ethical, medical, and literary thought. Anxieties about the natural capacities of the mind underlie and, in one sense at least, unify the intellectual projects of figures as otherwise diverse as Thomas Willis, the pioneer in anatomical studies of the brain; Thomas Sydenham, the most famous Restoration medic; Hobbes; Locke; Swift; and Sterne.[12] In referring to this broader context, I do not mean to detract or dilute what in this work is a specifically political focus. In fact, it is revealing how even for figures who are not considered political thinkers the imagination in particular has a conspicuous ethical and political gravity. This association ultimately has its roots in Aristotle and persists in the significance Hegel ascribed to it by linking imagination with subjectivity and "recognition."[13]

[12] One gets a sense of the significance and reach of the imagination as a troubling source of widespread anxiety from works such as Tuveson, *Imagination as a Means of Grace*, p. 16; Michael V. DePorte, *Nightmares and Hobbyhorses: Swift, Sterne and Augustan Ideas of Madness* (San Marino, Calif.: The Huntington Library, 1974); Ricardo Quintana, *Two Augustans* (Madison: University of Wisconsin Press, 1978); Michel Foucault, *Madness and Civilization*, trans. Richard Howard (New York: Vintage Books, 1988); and Amos Funkenstein, *Theology and the Scientific Imagination* (Princeton: Princeton University Press, 1986).

[13] Aristotle's discussion of imagination, which Hegel presents as his own starting point for a consideration of similar issues, is in Book 3 of *De Anima*. Hegel's reflections on imagination, subjectivity, and recognition are concentrated in the third part of *The Encyclopedia of Philosophic Sciences* and Chapter 3 of *The Phenomenology of Spirit*. For an interesting discussion of the importance of

My purpose in this chapter is to elaborate Locke's view of the natural tendencies of the mind. I do this by focusing mainly on his scattered remarks about curiosity and the imagination. With respect to the latter, since Locke himself associates it with madness, I am led to a consideration of the tenuous distinction separating madness from its opposite, along with the far-reaching moral and political implications this has for Locke. As becomes clear, the significance of madness in one sense lies in its revealing what is implicit in the very phenomena of the passions. For Locke, it is the passions, especially cognitive passions, that underlie behavior marked by an absence of self-control, an absence or obscurity of motive, all of which for Locke implies a disregard for the limits within which such behavior would remain efficacious. Broadly, two things define what is meant by efficacy in this context. First, it is that behavior that does not evince an absence of self-control and a similar inscrutablity of motive. But by itself this constraint does not, for Locke, establish a sufficiently narrow field of justified behavior. This occasions the second constraint, which refers to the positive valuation Locke places on submission, deference to conventional authority, and an acute concern with the reputational effects of behavior. I return to these considerations in Chapter 4 after the following discussion of the mind.

In focusing on the mind, I am not dealing with what is usually designated as Locke's philosophy of mind; rather, my focus is on the descriptive and adjectival details that accompany Locke's view of what the mind naturally tends to.

Curiosity and the "Busy Mind"

In the introduction to the *Essay Concerning Human Understanding*, Locke states his purpose as being

---

imagination in Hegel's thought, see John Sallis, "Imagination and Presentation in Hegel's Philosophy of Spirit," in *Hegel's Philosophy of Spirit*, ed. Peter. G. Stillman (Albany: State University of New York Press, 1987), pp. 66–88.

to inquire into the original, certainty and extent of human knowledge, together with the grounds and degrees of belief, opinion and assent . . . I shall not at present meddle with the physical consideration of the mind; or trouble myself to examine wherein its essence consists; or by what motions of our spirits or alterations of our bodies we came to have any sensations by our organs, or any ideas in our understanding; and whether those ideas do in their formation, . . . depend on matter or not. These are speculations which, however curious and entertaining, I shall decline, as lying out of my way in the design I am now upon. (*Essay*, p. 43)

Locke's inquiry into the "extent of human knowledge" is carefully structured to remain restricted to the "immediate objects" of the understanding. By refusing to "meddle with the physical consideration[s] of the mind" Locke frees himself of any concern with the relationship between ideas and whatever physical motions may be involved in their production. He is, in brief, refusing to go beyond the "appearances" of simple and mixed ideas. In doing so, he is refusing (and not just sidestepping, as Laslett would have it) to do what Hobbes had done.[14] Consider for instance the contrast between what Locke professes "as lying out of [his] way" and what Hobbes in the first chapter of the *Leviathan* concerns himself with: "The cause of Sense, is the External Body, or Object, which presseth the organ proper to each Sense, . . . which pressure, by the mediation of Nerves, and other strings, and membranes of the body, continued inwards to the Brain, the Heart, acauseth there a resistance, or counterpressure."[15] The variance is too poignant and too accurate not to be intended. It is equally significant. Whereas Hobbes tries to

---

[14] See Laslett's introduction to *Two Treatises*, p. 44: "Locke did not write . . . with Thomas Hobbes in hand or in mind, either to refute him or to adopt his doctrine without confessing it. Locke did not write as a philosopher, applying to politics the implications of his view of reality as a whole."

[15] Hobbes, *Leviathan*, p. 119.

pierce behind human appearance to reach his deductive starting point, Locke's point of theoretical departure is initiated by analytically limiting himself to "belief[s], opinion[s] and assent." Clearly Locke concern here sharply contrasts with the internalist focus on conscience evident in the *First Treatise*. By refusing to "meddle," Locke is slighting the disciplines that do not operate within limits. This is a charge with which he had rebuked Filmer for "huddling several suppositions together" of "general terms" (p. 173). Similarly, in marked contrast with Hobbes's deduction of passions by analysis of the "small beginnings of Motion, within the body of man, before they appears in visible actions,"[16] Locke identifies not a variety of motions but rather only "modes of pleasure and pain" (*Essay*, p. 229). His justification for this theoretical economy is to restate the epistemological limitation expressed at the beginning of the *Essay*. It is not, he announces, "my business here to inquire any further than into the bare ideas of our passions" (p. 230). Instead of Locke's inquiry into the bare ideas of passions, Hobbes, having identified pleasure (and pain) as "the appearance or sense of good," had to go behind this appearance to the "motion of Endeavor which consisteth in Appetite," and "appetite" was itself a complex motion, "a corroboration of Vitall motion, and help thereunto."[17]

It is this pervasive sense of setting methodological limits, and of binding his theoretical efforts to a context (I shall not *at present* . . . ; it is not my business *here* . . .), that reveals in Locke a narrow, though more intense, seriousness with which the individual to be "designed" becomes known.[18] It is worth recalling Locke's *First Treatise* critique of Filmer for extending his arguments too far and violating the context for which they were intended. It was an orientation in respect of which Filmer was

---

[16] Ibid.

[17] Hobbes, *Leviathan*, pp. 119–22.

[18] For a contrasting interpretation, see Peter A. Schouls, *The Imposition of Method* (Oxford: Clarendon Press, 1980).

characterized as mathematical, that is, of allowing his conclusions to be controlled by the abstraction implicit in his premises. Hobbes, I have suggested, is similarly viewed as representing a theoretical lack of control, of brandishing a theory without due concern for the limits within which its efficacy is bound. To designate this difference as simply one between Locke's methodological nominalism and Hobbes's corresponding absolutism would be to thoroughly miss the significance of Locke's critique. It is a significance which, as I have suggested with respect to Filmer, is profoundly linked to his political apprehension of the limitless, and hence threatening, potential of the subjectivity of human passions.[19]

The distinction between various subject matters and the cartographic identification of their respective boundaries is significant for another related reason. When Locke refuses to meddle with the physical aspects of the mind, declaring as out of the ambit of his concern all questions regarding human essence, bodily organs, motions, and the origin of sensation, he is restricting the area of anthropological curiosity to the human surface. His prohibitions, it must be emphasized, are not against studying and understanding human beings, still less are they a seventeenth-century throwback to Stoic *ataraxia*, with its dispassionate outlook on the world (*Nihil omnino agamus in vita;* We should do absolutely nothing in life). Nor is Locke, in the manner of Xenophon's Socrates, cautioning his curiosity against transgressing the boundary between matters human and matters scientific. On the contrary, Locke is calling attention to the study of human beings. But, in this distinctly modern prohibition, the cautioning boundary has people on both sides of it. More precisely, the study must restrain itself against its own overexertion,

---

[19] Locke's methodological restrictions on curiosity are strikingly similar to John Calvin's prohibitions. In this, as in his ambivalent attitude toward conscience, Locke is drawing on a Calvinistic legacy. See Michael Walzer, *The Revolution of the Saints* (New York: Atheneum, 1972), pp. 22–35.

that is, against penetrating too deeply into the object of its curiosity. At the level of cognitive appetite this restraint takes the form of instructing a "busy mind" to

> be more cautious in meddling with things exceeding its comprehension; to stop when *it* is at the utmost extent of *its* tether; and sit down in quiet ignorance of those things, which upon examination, are found to be beyond the reach of our capacities. We should not then perhaps be so forward out of an affection of an universal knowledge, to raise questions, and perplex ourselves and others with disputes about things to which our understandings are not suited; and . . . learn to content ourselves with what is attainable by us *in this state.* (*Essay*, pp. 44–45, emphasis added)

The appetite for knowledge must curb itself from extending, not into a divine sphere where it would face a Promethean rebuke, but rather from a sphere in which it will perplex itself. The temptation to overstep boundaries stems not from an external seduction but from the tendency to go beyond the reach of our own capacities. It is a "quarrel with [our] own constitution" that threatens the "busy mind." The cognitive drive of the mind cannot presume that all cognitive achievement will "be of use to us." It is the simultaneous accenting human capacities and their in-built dangers which distinguish Locke's prohibitions from the millennium of Christian restrictions that preceded him. It is not a "despair of knowing anything" in the face of an omniscient Author but rather a danger of "question[ing] everything" (p. 46).

The mind's quest for knowledge, indeed the mind's quest for anything, must be viewed with a caution appropriate to an entity that can trip itself up or, to change the metaphor, effortlessly lead itself into a labyrinthian maze. Like the body, the mind must be viewed with constant vigilance. Locke is aware of a problem here, a problem akin to trying to become aware of one's visual capacities by using the eyes. To this problem, the only solution is to mold the mind before it becomes self-conscious, to clip its excesses before they become inconveniently and incorrigibly linked with the transgressive will (or conception of freedom) of an individual, and this can be done only in a very young child. I consider this matter at greater length in the next chapter.

Locke's persistent effort is to bind the mind's natural and tenacious curiosity, to link or anchor it in some particular purpose. Consider the following remark from *Of the Conduct of the Understanding*, which was to be the longest part of the *Essay*, the title of which is itself suggestive of my point: "The eagerness and strong bent of the mind after knowledge, if not warily regulated, is often a hindrance to it. It still presses into further discoveries and new objects and catches at the variety of knowledge . . . for haste to pursue what is yet out of sight."[20] What saves such a remark from self-contradiction (what would curiosity be if it were not the pursuit of something out of sight?) is that it is directed at the haste of the mind, and not at the simple fact of its curiosity. Later in the same section (the section is entitled "Haste"), Locke says,

> There is another haste that does often and will mislead the mind, if it be left to itself and its own conduct. The understanding is naturally forward, not only to learn its knowledge by variety (which makes it skip over one to get speedily to another part of knowledge), but also eager to enlarge its views by running too fast into general observations and conclusions without a due examination of particulars enough whereon to found those general axioms. This seems to enlarge their stock, but is of fancies not realities.[21]

What Locke is referring to is a natural haste in the mind, a tendency it evinces if left to its own conduct. Later, he explicitly

[20] John Locke, *Of the Conduct of the Understanding*, ed. F. W. Garforth (New York: Teacher's College Press, 1966), p. 86.
[21] Ibid., p. 87.

links this tendency with the power to overturn all morality and undermine every shred of order. The mind is in desperate need of husbanding. It cannot be left to its own natural proclivities. Even when these proclivities incline it to an understanding or curiosity of the beatific vision "of the other life," this concern with salvation is to be limited, if not denied, at the level of the mind: "This I am sure, the principle end why we are to get knowledge here is to make use of it for the benefit of ourselves and others in this world."[22]

It is a split in curiosity that makes it both the original driving power in the potentially unlimited pretensions of humankind, with its apparently cumulative mastery of reality, and also the grounds whereby this process threatens to rebound and subvert itself. It was suggested earlier that in substituting the settled Filmerian understanding of faith by the inscrutable though volatile category of conscience, Locke had signaled the transfer of his focus onto an individual of vastly expanded concerns. The "busy mind" belongs to this individual. It represents in Locke's view the infinite pretensions of a finite entity caught in the chaotic traffic of its own cogitations. It is what makes Locke embarrassingly but also unmistakably suspicious of the very idea of infinity in the *Essay*,[23] about which he states "that things infinite are too large for our capacities; we can have no comprehensive knowledge of them, and our thoughts are at a loss, and confounded when we pry too curiously into them" (*Thoughts*, p. 420). This is not the humility of a man confronted with the vast unending abundance of things to be known; nor is it a self-confident indifference stemming from the recognition that the world and knowledge of it are not organized for his understanding. Instead, Locke shows a vivid sense of timidity verging on fear that our own minds may be confounded and put at a loss by

[22] John Locke, *Some Thoughts Concerning Education*, ed. James Axtell (Cambridge: Cambridge University Press, 1968), p. 412. Hereafter cited as *Thoughts*.
[23] Locke, *Essay*, Bk. II, chap. 17. See in particular the latter half of the chapter.

the excesses of our curiosity. This is an outlook that needs to order and organize not just external things but the mind itself, to give it an internal stability in the absence of this being part of its natural endowment. Nothing, I believe, better captures this admixture of anxiety and the corresponding need for self-prescribed order than the following passage from the conclusion of the *Thoughts:*

> For shortening our pains, and keeping us from incurable doubt and perplexity of mind and an endless inquiry after greater certainty than is to be had . . . it would be very convenient . . . to consider what proofs the matter in hand is capable of, and not to expect other kinds of evidence than the nature of the thing will bear. . . . I have avoided confusion in my thoughts; the scheme I had made serving like a regular chest of drawers to lodge those things orderly and in their proper places which came to hand confusedly. (Pp. 420–21)

To the possible perplexity of the mind, Locke's own personal response was to carve out in his own mind orderly slots that would, in the absence of a natural order of things, keep things neatly compartmentalized. But this classificatory system, this "regular chest of drawers," is not simply the mind's response to a world in which the Great Chain of Being has collapsed onto itself. Rather, it is a response in which the mind is deemed to be devoid of internal and natural pigeonholes and thus in danger of being culled into an endless inquiry—an inquiry which some may call curiosity but which Locke views as manifesting a pathological condition in which the mind is without anchor.

Nowhere are Locke's views more at odds with the major figures of the seventeenth century than in the dangers he perceives and restrictions he suggests to the unbounded curiosity of the mind. In contrast with Francis Bacon's battle cry to experimental science, *plus ultra,* we have Locke's sedentary injunction to sit down in quiet ignorance of those things beyond our reach.

Whereas Descartes places his hopes for an ideal knowledge in geometry, the *sominium de reductione scientiae ad geometriam* (the dream to reduce science to geometry),[24] Locke endorses mathematics not on the basis of its enormous potential but only to the degree that it makes us more "reasonable creatures."[25] In contrast to Hobbes's unleashing of curiosity (if guided by the "orderly Method in proceeding from the Elements, which are Names to Assertions made by Connexion of one of them to another; and so to Syllogisms, which are the Connexions of one Assertions to another, till we come to a knowledge of all the Consequences"),[26] we have Locke's denunciation of such methodological single-mindedness "that is the hunting after arguments to make good one side of a question and wholly to neglect and refuse those which favor the other side."[27]

There is something obviously disturbing about Locke's theoretical restraint, his muted enthusiasm to join in the chorus of celebration that accompanies the modern age's most cherished interpretation of itself as an age of reason, as an epoch of unbounded curiosity. "To sit in quiet ignorance": was that not precisely the view of humanity in the Middle Ages against which the seventeenth century had congratulated itself for its theoretical vigor and intellectual capaciousness? It is further unsettling to our familiar historical picture to note that in the century that preferred to view Doctor Faustus's cognitive appetite not as a sinful encroachment but rather as a form of tragic greatness[28] Locke was still "search[ing] out the bounds between opinion and knowledge" (*Essay*, p. 44). From this kind of cautiousness Locke's nineteenth-century critics were able to perpetuate the image of

---

[24] Quoted from Alexandre Koyré, "Newton and Descartes," in *Newtonian Studies* (Cambridge: Harvard University Press, 1965), p. 53.

[25] Locke, *Conduct*, p. 49.

[26] Hobbes, *Leviathan*, p. 115.

[27] Locke, *Conduct*, p. 67.

[28] Blumenberg, *Legitimacy of the Modern Age*, pp. 381–83.

him as lacking "philosophical largess of view" and having "origi-
nated little or nothing."[29]

Notwithstanding this view, we must look more closely at the
mind against whose extravagances Locke was expressing a lonely
voice of dissent. My concern is with the descriptive details that
accompany and hold the mind together and thus point to its
natural tendencies. In dealing with Locke's understanding of the
mind, we are dealing with an entity that is still in need of careful
attention. We cannot assume, as Locke himself did not, that its
signification is settled. In its usage, the word "mind" is carefully padded by adjectival qualifications and integrated within
graphic images. In short, it demands from the author (and the
reader) an attentiveness that must be sensitive to the fluid yet
confident provenance of its meaning. In speaking of the mind we
are, after all, speaking of an entity which, as Richard Rorty has
suggested, was invented only as recently as Descartes.[30]

At the beginning of Book II of the *Essay*, having introduced his
famous simile of the mind as "white paper void of all characters,
without any ideas," Locke asks the following question: "Whence
comes it by that vast store which the busy and boundless fancy
of man has painted on it with an almost endless variety?" To this
question, Locke gives his famous "one-word" answer, "from
EXPERIENCE" (p. 104). The answer is given greater poignancy if
we consider what is taken for granted in the question. Locke's
formulation of the question is made from the position that takes

[29] William Whewell, *Philosophy of the Inductive Sciences* (1840), and in *Lectures on
the History of Moral Philosophy in England*, quoted in Aarsleff, "Locke's Reputation," p. 409. It should be noted that, although Whewell's view was, as Aarsleff
suggests, a popular one, it was not altogether a prominent one. Both the Mill's,
for instance, thought of themselves as belonging to the "school of Locke"; see
"Coleridge," in Mill's *Essays on Literature and Society*, ed. J. B. Schneewind (New
York: Collier Books, 1965), p. 302; and Robert D. Cumming, *Human Nature and
History* (Chicago: University of Chicago Press, 1969), 2:113–41.

[30] Richard Rorty, *Philosophy and the Mirror of Nature* (Princeton: Princeton
University Press, 1979), pp. 17–68.

as given that the mind is a *vast* store, that it is the repository of a *busy* and *boundless fancy*, and which, moreover, is capable of almost *endless* variety. None of these expansive adjectives stands in need of justification; they all accompany the mind, silently attending to it as though mere facts. Locke goes on to announce and distinguish the two "fountains of knowledge" from which our ideas do spring—sensation and reflection. Having done so, he returns almost immediately to the theme of the mind's expansiveness: "How great a mass of knowledge . . . be lodged in [this] mind . . . with infinite variety compounded and enlarged by the understanding." Even the mind of a child is "perpetually and diversely affect[ed]"; lights and colors being "busy at hand everywhere" the eye cannot resist them as they "force an entrance to the mind." The mind may be helpless against sensory intrusions, but it is not for that reason wholly passive. Indeed, Locke constantly emphasizes how the mind is made more busy by "its own operations," how "when . . . [it] is once stored with these simple ideas, it has the power to repeat, compare, and unite them, even to an almost infinite variety" (pp. 124–26). The picture is that of a mind bombarded by external stimuli and further multiplied by its own enthusiasm. In the *Conduct of the Understanding*, Locke makes explicit reference to this characterization of the mind in a section entitled "Wandering." His purpose here is to underscore the "constant succession and flux of ideas in our mind" and point to the difficulty in "get[ting] that power over our minds as to be able to direct that train of ideas."[31] In fact, in this particular section Locke, with uncharacteristic resignation, suggests that he knows of no easy way to rein in the mind and would instead gladly listen to one who knew.

Underlying these and various similar statements is a simple, even if deeply troubling, conviction—that we do not anywhere near fully control the ideas and combinations of ideas that enter

[31] Locke, *Conduct*, p. 94.

the mind and effect its inclinations. Stemming from this lack of control one can say, as so many of Locke's formulations suggest, that we are in danger of being controlled by these unsteady, unpredictable, and in principle unlimited mental profusions. A vivid and concise sense of these threatening tendencies is revealed in a manuscript in the Lovelace collection titled "Of Study": "There is a kind of restiness in almost everyone's mind; sometimes without perceiving the cause, it will boggle and stand still, and one cannot get it to step forward; and at other times it will press forward and there is no holding it in."[32] Locke's language, by referring to the mind in the personified form, underscores the sense of being controlled by this *it*, with *its* intractable volition, *its* capacity to lead us without limit, and *its* equally inscrutable grounds for immobilizing us in our tracks.

Madness and the Imagination

Before concluding this chapter, I want to consider Locke's views on madness. These are striking for two reasons. First, they have all but escaped the attention of recent Locke scholars. Not only have they not been discussed, but their perceived insignificance has resulted in their being expunged from the various abridged versions of Locke's published journals and texts. Locke's journal entries dealing with passions, interest, and reason were of sufficient interest to W. von Leyden to be selected for publication, but, despite Locke's stated connection of these to madness, the latter were left out. Similarly, Aaron and Gibb, like John Gough, completely overlooked Locke's discussion of madness.[33]

[32] Locke, *Thoughts*, appendix 4, MS Locke f.2, p. 414.
[33] John Locke, *Essays on the Law of Nature*; John Locke, *An Early Draft of Locke's Essay Together with Excerpts from His Journal*, ed. R. I. Aaron and Jocelyn Gibb (Oxford: Clarendon Press, 1936); John Locke, *Locke's Travels in France, 1675–1679*, ed. John Gough (Cambridge: Cambridge University Press, 1953).

These sustained omissions are made more striking by the fact that Locke's interest in madness cannot be designated as a merely private fascination that therefore had to be relegated to his cryptic journals. In fact, Locke discusses madness in all his major published works; indeed, in the case of the *Essay Concerning Human Understanding*, the sections dealing with madness are substantially supplemented in later editions.[34]

My second reason for considering Locke's views on madness is that they reveal with unmistakable clarity two significant features of the mind which point to the larger political ramifications I am urging regarding the importance of cognitive considerations. The first is that distinctions between the normal and the pathological, those to be politically included within consensual politics and those who must live in a condition of permanent tutelage—in brief, those who can consent and those who must simply be governed—turn on considerations of the mind. The second is that the features of the mind these distinctions turn on are themselves common to both sides of the distinction and therefore do not constitute clear mental, ontological, biological, or natural markers. The mind is thus an ambivalent site that must nevertheless support unambiguous political distinctions. In the next chapter, I consider Locke's response to this predicament. In the present, it is worth making clear that when Locke, at the outset of the *Essay*, announces that his purpose with respect to the mind is "to examine our own Abilities, and see, what Objects our Understandings were, or were not fitted to deal with" (p. 7), he is, after all, centrally concerned with examining the extent to which our powers are suitable to life in the commonwealth. If this examination were to suggest a diagnosis in which the mind was afflicted with an almost pathological urge

---

[34] In the fourth edition of the *Essay*, Locke inserted the chapter "Of the Association of Ideas," in which, while speaking of madness, he states: "There is scarse a Man so free from it" (p. 395).

toward indiscriminate transgression; if, moreover, in its curiosity it was blind to the efficacy of what it searched into; and if, finally, it was helpless in prescribing limits for itself—then perhaps the commonwealth within which it was to be situated would have to assume many of the strictures common to a hospital, perhaps to those of an asylum. If, on the other hand, the pathology of the mind stemmed not from a biological helplessness but rather from a lack of due concern while it was being nurtured, then the commonwealth would, perhaps, share some of the attributes of a rehabilitation and remedial center. In either event there are, I think, prima facie grounds that should give the views on madness by a theorist so obsessed with limits a political poignancy.

In the first chapter of *Madness and Civilization*, Foucault speaks of the revival of the great mythic themes surrounding the Ship of Fools. Both as a literary composition and as a navigational fact, the rivers and seas of Europe appear in the fifteenth and sixteenth centuries to be carrying a considerable amount of insane cargo. Instead of being allowed to live a semi-human existence at the outskirts of the city, madmen are quite simply banished. Their voyage "is at once a rigorous division and an absolute passage."[35] In this need for a radical separation, one senses the mutually threatening proximity of the sane and the insane. The settled hierarchy of vices through which the Middle Ages had comfortably designated and lived with madness are by this time clearly in need of redefinition and support. The interjection of an unmistakable physical distance between the sane and the insane reflects and foreshadows an emerging psychological ambivalence which, by the seventeenth century and certainly with Locke, acquires an acuteness thereby rendering the physical metaphor of the *Stultifera navis* thoroughly inadequate.

In an early journal entry from his stay in France, Locke

---

[35] Foucault, *Madness and Civilization*, p. 11, see pp. 3–38.

queries himself "whether madness be not the wrong application of mad ideas to things that exist, but are neither having of wrong ideas nor wrong reasoning, and then so that it seems to exist wholly in proposition into simple ideas or syllogisms, as for example [those] made in phantasy [such as] him to be either king or candle."[36] The language may be equivocal and inconclusive but the very terms around which Locke equivocates are radical for what they neglect. Whatever else madness may be, it is not, as it had been, a lack of charity, an excess of pride, a neglect of Christian virtues, or a fixation with stigmatizing vices.[37] The tentative view that madness may be "made in phantasy" is, a little over a year later, given definitive authority. On 5 November 1677, Locke notes in his journal "Madnesse seems to be noething but a disorder in the imagination, and not in the discursive faculty; for one shall find amongst the distract, those who phansy them selves kings, and, who discourse and reason right enough upon the suppositions and wrong phansys they have taken.[38] Madness, far from being a condition of discursive deficiency, is a state in which the mind is consumed in an overexcited frenzy of activity. Its regal pretensions indicate nothing sinful or sedentary but rather an extravagant imaginative profusion. Nor is the mind's logical capacity impaired and, if the mad are unreasonable, they are so only because they appear distracted by their own cogitating excesses. Nor is this condition an exceptional one, characterizing only a few shiploads of people who could conveniently be carted off to sea; as Locke goes on to say, it is a state which "any sober man may find . . . in himself" and which

---

[36] From Locke's medical notes and journal, cited in Kenneth Dewhurst, *John Locke (1632–1704) Physician and Philosopher: A Medical Biography* (London: Wellcome Historical Medical Library, 1963), p. 71, journal entry dated 22 July 1676. This is, I think, the only book in English that has Locke's entries regarding madness, albeit in abridged form.

[37] Foucault, *Madness and Civilization*, p. 13.

[38] Dewhurst, *John Locke*, journal entry 5 November 1677, p. 89.

"most people may have observed to have happened to themselves."[39] By freeing madness from the profusion of Gothic and
Christian symbolism, Locke gives it a clinical simplicity. But,
ironically, this simplicity itself makes possible an alternative
proliferation of meaning from a self-generating network of associations and significations. The imaginative fancies of a mad
mind, once set in motion, have no conceivable limit and face no
natural constraint. Meanings, one might say, lose the stabilizing
support they ordinarily get from things or, more precisely, from
the memory of things. Once the animating force of reason becomes merely the "suppositions" and "wrong phansys" of the
imagination, a gap opens in which the "sober man" and the
madman are in danger of being indistinguishable.

With respect to a fixed moral hierarchy, the mad and sober
minds have lost their differentiating locations, and in their syllogistic capacity they appear equally adept. What then distinguishes them? Alternatively, what stops madness from invading
the territory from which it had, until recently, been banished?

On 22 January 1678, Locke made a long entry in his journal.
The entry bore two titles in the margin. The first was "Memory," the second "Madness." The discussion of these two topics
is, however, continuous despite the marginalia. Mirroring his
language from the discussion of simple and complex ideas in the
Essay, Locke states,

> When we revive in our mindes the Idea of anything that we
> have before observed to exist this we call memory. . . . But
> when from the observation we have made of divers particulars
> we make a general idea to represent any species in general as a
> man, or else joyne several ideas together which we never
> observed to exist together we call it Imagination. Soe that
> memory is always the picture of some thing the Idea of whereof
> hath existed before in our thoughts as neare the life as we can

39 Ibid.

draw it. But Imagination is a picture drawne in our mind without reference to a patterne.[40]

The mind, while guided by memory, is fixed on an observed object or, in Locke's revealing image, it is literally "tied to a patterne."[41] Even though the mind can never perfectly apprehend this "originall," the very knowledge of its existence serves as an epicenter around which it disciplines its thought. Stated in its more popular form, the mind, in trying to draw an Idea as close to a live object, tries to obtain more and more accurate representations of that object. This, of course, is the nub of Locke's allegedly empirical epistemology—for which, beginning at least with Thomas Reid, he has often been criticized. The most usual criticism is simply that Locke assumes that, in the relationship between an object and the internal idea of it, an actual impression is made by the former, thus making possible the latter. This involves what Sellars refers to as the attempt to "analyze epistemic facts without remainder into nonepistemic facts,[42] and what T. H. Green calls "the fundamental confusion . . . between two essentially distinct questions—one metaphysical, What is the simplest element of knowledge? the other physiological, What are the conditions in the individual human organism in virtue of which it becomes a vehicle of knowledge?"[43] The validity of this often-cited charge cannot be denied. Locke, like Aristotle, did think of knowledge as a relationship between a person and an object. The simile of a wax tablet being impressed by objects was, I think, meant quite literally.

If the validity of this criticism cannot be denied, it does not,

---

[40] Ibid., 22 January 1678, p. 100.

[41] Ibid., p. 101.

[42] Wilfrid Sellars, *Science, Perception, and Reality* (New York: Humanities Press, 1963), p. 131.

[43] T. H. Green, *Hume and Locke*, ed. Ramon Lemos (New York: Crowell, 1968), pp. 131–64. Also see Rorty, *Philosophy and the Mirror of Nature*.

nevertheless, fully capture Locke's purpose. Specifically, it over-looks the sense in which Locke speaks of ideas apprehending objects as a way of disciplining or tying the mind down. In the passage just quoted Locke admits that our ideas can only "draw neare" the object without ever perfectly "picturing" it; yet, de-spite this fundamental limit to our knowledge of the object, Locke commends memory in contrast to the imagination. He says in the entry to which I have just referred:

> I think that haveing often recourse to ones memory and tieing down the minde strictly to the recollecting of things past precisely as they were may be a meanes to *check those extrava-gant turning flights of the imagination*. And tis good often to divert the minde from that which it had been earnestly im-ploied about, or which is its ordinary business to other objects, and make it attend to the information of the senses and the things they offer to it. [44]

The language is striking. The mind, while trying to strictly recollect the sensory impression made on it, is "tied down," and its "extravagance" is kept in "check." Moreover, in attending to the information of the senses it is "diverted" from the flights of the imagination. In an earlier journal entry Locke similarly com-mends the focus on impressions as a way to settle the mind, or else "all our meditations and discourse . . . will be noe thing but perfect raveing."[45] Locke is emphasizing the importance of at-tending to sensory impressions, but he does not encourage this on the grounds of its epistemological infallibility. Instead, he focuses on sensory attentiveness explicitly because such atten-tion serves, in his view, as a diversion from and anchor against the potential ravings of the imagination.

---

[44] Dewhurst, *John Locke*, journal entry 22 January 1678, Journals, pp. 101–2.
[45] Ibid., 5 November 1677, p. 89. Likewise, in *Conduct*, p. 95, Locke points to the importance of sensory pursuits as a means of "keep[ing] [our thoughts] from taking off."

One cannot overlook the political significance of this empirical or sensory emphasis. The contrast between madness and its opposite (a term that Locke with prophetic restraint never firmly christens) has lost the absolute dichotomy available to a previous mode of thinking in terms of the opposition between Satan and Christ or vice and virtue. In speaking of madness Locke inherits a tradition that is analogically bankrupt. The contrast can be maintained, but it does not turn on any natural categories, rather only on the degree of success in restraining or disciplining the imagination—which itself is a natural feature of the mind. The challenge presented by the imagination is clearly in its implications a political one. But it is in the nature of the imagination as Locke understands it that it can be disciplined only by very early habituation, and hence the challenge is translated by Locke into an issue of early childhood education. All that distinguishes the mad from their opposites is the *extent* of the former's imagination and the corresponding disregard to limit themselves by the recollection of sensory impressions. And, if this distinction is too thin and too vague to give us the comfortable security of not being mad, Locke at least is fully aware of the curious equality of madness he has uncovered.

In the chapter "Of the Association of Ideas" which was appended to the fourth edition of the *Essay*, Locke begins by claiming that "there is scarce any one that does not observe something that is in it self really Extravagant in the Opinions, Reasonings, and Actions of other Men." This great "Unreasonableness" of which we are all "guilty," Locke goes on to suggest, cannot be wholly understood as a form of "self-love," nor can it simply be ascribed to a paucity of education or an excess of prejudice. It is in fact a "sort of Madness" that "has its Original in very sober and rational Minds." Fully aware of the ramifications of what he has just suggested, Locke immediately goes on to ask his readers' pardon for the use of so harsh a name as madness, but he notes that he is bound to his word since "there is scarce a Man so free from it" (*Essay*, pp. 394–95). He emphasizes the sincerity of his apology for imputing madness "on the greatest part of mankind" but, after carefully inquiring into the nature of madness, he has "found it to spring from the very same Root, and to depend on the very same Cause" as reasonableness. It is, he goes on, "a Weakness to which all men are so liable [and] which so universally infects mankind," which moreover "is of so great [a] force to set us awry in our Actions, as well Moral as Natural Passions, Reasonings, and Notions themselves, that, perhaps, there is not any one thing that deserves more to be looked after" (p. 397). Locke explicitly denies that this condition or susceptibility to this condition is limited to those "under the power of an unruly passion." In this denial he distinguishes his own understanding of madness from that of Hobbes, who also links it with the imagination. But for Hobbes, madness refers merely to the exceptional circumstances in which people are overcome by a particular passion, such as pride, and where as a result they are led to counterprudential behavior. One redress to this situation for Hobbes is to counter such passions with other passions, such as fear and terror, which leads to disciplining the effects of the former.[46] In contrast, for Locke the excesses of the imagination stem simply from the perfectly natural tendency of the mind to combine ideas and to do so in strange ways. It is only with very few ideas that there exists a "natural correspondence and connection one with another." For the rest, the associations the mind generates stem from chance, "different inclinations, education, interests" (pp. 395–96). Even the distinct interests of human beings cannot exhaustively explain the associations they develop. In the face of this fertile and febrile imagination, the "reason" even of "men of sincerity" is blinded.

[46] See Hobbes, *Leviathan*, chap. 8. For an interesting and brief discussion of Hobbes's and other seventeenth-century views of madness, see DePorte, *Nightmares and Hobbyhorses*, pp. 3–48. I have benefited from an unpublished paper of Joshua Cohen's in understanding Hobbes's views on the passions and madness.

In the chapter on "Discerning" in the *Essay*, Locke summarizes his thoughts on madness while contrasting this condition with that of idiots. The latter suffer from "the want and weakness of any or all faculties." Madmen, in contrast, "do not appear . . . to have lost the faculty of reasoning: but having joined together some ideas very wrongly, they mistake them for truths; and they err as men do that argue right from wrong principles. For by the violence of their imaginations, having taken their fancies for realities, they make right deductions from them" (p. 161). When Locke says that the ideas and their associations are *wrong* in madmen, he is in fact expressing a strong conviction for which his own theorizing gives him only tenuous grounds. Locke himself points to how in all the operations of the mind, such as abstraction, discernment, or comparison, the mad are, in principle, no less adept than their counterparts. The imagination, like reason, simply is not a faculty limited to the mad.

Locke has divested madness of the mist of contorted allusions and morally condemnatory associations. There is no hierarchy of vices, no mention of strange spirits, internal humors, hallucinations, manias, secret lustful desires, and hence no corresponding need for severe chastisement, blood letting, special potions, extended sentences in extreme cold or heat. All this has been dispensed with. In fact, it is surprising that Locke the medic should not have felt a greater need to interpret madness through some residual medical vocabulary. It is also surprising that Locke, the pious Christian, should have viewed the "enthusiasms" of his fellow Christians as no more than a form of madness in which the delusions of unmediated divine communication are little more than the "conceits of a warmed or overweening brain" that has been overtaken by the imagination (p. 699). But then none of this is surprising, because for Locke madness "springs from the very same root" as its sober counterpart and thus its instances are often found in precincts surprisingly close to those designated as normal. Precisely for this reason again, Locke's madmen cannot be carted off to sea or confined in asylums or penitentiaries. Madness is a ubiquitous potentiality and hence, in one very general and politically decisive sense, is not a special condition at all.

Consider Locke's words as he speaks of the "pure effects of [the] imagination":

> This at least is the cause of great errors and mistakes amongst men when [the imagination] does not wholly unhinge the braines and put all government of the thoughts into the hands of the imagination as it sometimes happens, when the imagination by being much imploid and getting the mastry about any one thing usurps the dominion over all the other facultys of the minde . . . [and] gives it on such an occasion that empire.[47]

Madness has clearly ceased to be the sign of another world. The province it usurps is not inhabited by strange fauna, lurking spirits, and devouring monsters. The threat of being subjugated by the empire of madness stems from its prevailing normality. Imaginative excess and a strange association of ideas are all that it takes to unhinge the sobriety of the mind and shatter the government of the thoughts.

The highly political language that carries through in the passage just cited has a double significance. It reveals, on the one hand, how the metaphor for understanding the unhinged mind is thoroughly political—the thoughts when they lose their government are usurped by the imagination, thereby surrendering the other faculties to the threat of a mental imperialism. But, on the other hand, Locke's language suggests how madness has become a threatening metaphor for a politics unhinged. If the excesses of the imagination render the mind mad and without government, can we escape the implicit inference that the excesses of political passions would perhaps render politics curi-

---

[47] Dewhurst, *John Locke*, journal entry, 22 January 1678, p. 101, emphasis added.

ously demented too? And since madness threatens the mind by instigating an excess imminent in its natural condition, can we avoid the suggestion that the passions in their natural state are susceptible to a similar excess and hence liable to a similar threat? Put differently, in uncovering the mind's tendency toward a cogitating excess—an excess that issues in a madness that could "overturn all morality," have we not arrived at the principle whereby the exercise of the passions in the state of nature transforms that state into the state of war?

The distinction between madness and its counterpart cannot be firmly designated in terms of the faculties of the mind. What gives this absence its real significance is that it speaks to another, politically more familiar distinction, namely, that between freedom and license (*Second Treatise*, pp. 288–89). This distinction Locke associates with the presence or absence of reason. Freedom, we are told, requires a law to guide it, and that law is reason. But what becomes clear from the discussion of madness is that the mad (i.e., potentially and occasionally anyone and everyone) have all the requisite faculties for reason and, hence one would assume, for freedom. Indeed, the mad satisfy even the conditions requisite for freedom as Locke presents them in the chapter on power in the *Essay*. They can suspend their desires and judgments, and can subject them to a discriminating will. Madness, after all, is a condition pertaining to the imagination and the associations generated by it; it is not a condition of total lack of self-control.

In following through with the puzzlement regarding what distinguishes madness from its counterpart, we are led to ask, on what basis does Locke explicitly exclude the mad from the consensual politics of the *Second Treatise*? (pp. 325–26). In asking this question in the present context, I am not pursuing an interest in questions of exclusion, but rather in the question of what distinguishes freedom from license and hence what constitutes the reason that is the basis of freedom. Depending on Locke's answer to this question, we will know who precisely he has in mind when he excludes mad people from consensual politics. What description of human beings fits Locke's conception of the mad when he speaks of their necessary exclusion? This question, of course, bears on the larger query about the basis and need for political society.

In the chapter on power in the *Essay*, Locke considers the following question: "Is it worth the name of freedom to be at liberty to play the fool, and draw shame and misery upon a man's self? If to break loose from the conduct of reason, and to want that restraint of examination and judgment, which keeps us from choosing and doing the worse, be liberty, true liberty, madmen and fools are the only free men" (p. 265). The question is itself significant because it makes clear that there are conditions attached to the efficacy of freedom. The contrast between the liberty chosen by madmen and fools and the liberty which, if Locke were not being sarcastic, he would call true liberty is that the latter presumably ensures the avoidance of shame and misery. This is a gratuitous claim because Locke's examples more often than not suggest that madness is not a condition that leads to self-inflicted misery or pain (e.g., thinking oneself a king or a candle). But it does invariably result in shame or scorn stemming from the condition and "normal" perspective of those who view and judge it. From the standpoint of the madperson, such reputational costs may be of no consequence if nevertheless he or she is allowed to do and express what he or she has freely chosen. Locke ignores this possibility, even though in a sense he signals its presence by the reference that links freedom with an absence of shame. In the next chapter, I draw out more fully both the extent and the depth to which freedom, reason, and reputation are linked for Locke. In the present context, my point is simply to emphasize that, when Locke speaks, as he does so often, of freedom involving the guidance of reason, the reason he has in mind is quite specific. It is reason informed by a particular substantive content and one deeply invested in and extremely sensitive to conventional norms of acceptability.

The madperson, with his or her imagination—an imagination that may lead him or her to think him or herself a king and queen, with strange bodies and stranger fantasies, and yet with perfectly good discursive and syllogistic capacities—shatters the settled and conventionally secure associations of Locke's timid reason. Their reason, let us call it subjective, does not need the guidance, the tutelage, or ultimately the governance of another reason to be free. Or perhaps it is governed by a different conception of reason, perhaps it is tutored but by a different teacher, perhaps it is guided but by a different light and destination. Perhaps it is just different. And perhaps it is the threat of this difference, a difference that may take many forms, that Locke senses in the madperson and to ensure against which his politics is, in one sense, directed. In that event, the freedom, the rationality, and the equality Locke celebrates and on which he bases liberal politics is not the natural freedom, the natural rationality, or the natural equality of human beings, but rather a carefully crafted artifice framed with reference to a particular vision of society and the individuals who inhabit it.[48] In this crafting, there is a strange timidity, for it does not vindicate itself in the conflict and dialogue between two rival freedoms, two rival rationalities—one mad, the other professing sanity. In-

[48] I think this resistance to difference is what Foucault has in mind when, in the preface to *Madness and Civilization* (p. 12), he writes: "We have yet to write the history of that other form of madness, by which men, in an act of sovereign reason, confine their neighbors, and communicate and recognize each other through the merciless language of non-madness; to define the moment of this conspiracy before it was permanently established in the realm of truth, before it was revived by the lyricism of protest. We must try to return, in history, to that zero point in the course of madness at which madness is an undifferentiated experience, a not yet divided experience of division itself. We must describe, from the start of its trajectory, that 'other form' which relegates Reason and Madness to one side or the other of its action as things henceforth external, deaf to all exchange, and as though dead to one another."

stead, it is directed at an infant before he or she has "reason, reflection or memory" with which to counterpose and perhaps resist the effects of this molding. It is to this artificing that I turn in the next chapter.

For Locke as for the madperson it is the imagination and the status accorded to it that ultimately determines the political destiny of what it means to be different. The fact that the madperson and the imagination can serve as a mirror on the larger questions of individuality and political order is testimony to the simple point that it is through the imagination that we (not just the madperson) fantasize, and it is our fantasies that effect our values, our interests, our commitments, and hence the particular content of our freedom. All this Locke understood long before it was commonplace. But in his response to this recognition is evident a pusillanimity of vision and a weakness of nerve in what different imaginings and fantasies may bring forth. Locke places his stamp on subsequent forms of liberalism both in the noble insight that links imagination with freedom and, unfortunately, in the urge to circle the wagons and close itself off from different imaginations that it cannot comprehend or otherwise tolerate.

CHAPTER FOUR

Molding Individuality:
Direction and Compromise

Man is not fitted for society by nature, but by discipline
—Thomas Hobbes

The focus of this chapter is Locke's largely neglected *Some Thoughts Concerning Education*. The work comprises a series of letters Locke wrote at the request of his friend Edward Clarke to facilitate the education of Clarke's son. These letters were published in book form during Locke's lifetime and, even though Locke characteristically withheld revealing his authorship from the title page of the first edition, he did acknowledge it in the "Epistle" and thus appears to have been less reluctant and evasive to see this work in print than he was for most of his other books. The fact that education was deeply important to Locke and that its importance, in great measure, turned on moral and political considerations is vividly evident in the text and from the biographical details of his life.[1]

In the present context, I want to point to the significance of education for Locke by reference to two theoretical problematics. The first derives from the discussion of the mind and more specifically of the imagination examined in the previous chapter.

---

[1] See, for example, *Thoughts*, pp. 3–88. Also see Nathan Tarcov, *Locke's Education for Liberty* (Chicago: University of Chicago Press, 1984), pp. 1–8; Maurice Cranston, *John Locke: A Biography* (London: Longmans, Green, 1957).

The second, although ultimately also linked with considerations of the mind, is framed by reference to Locke's understanding of natural freedom, reason, and the laws of nature, and hence it follows directly from the *Two Treatises*.

Let me begin by considering the latter of these two problematics. On the face of it, Locke's claim that human beings are naturally free is puzzling; it is elaborated in terms of conventional possibilities for such freedom *and* of various preconventional obligations human beings are bound by. Thus, at the outset of the *Second Treatise*, he states that "all men are naturally in . . . a *state of perfect freedom* to order their actions, and dispose of their possessions, and persons as they think fit, within the bounds of the law of nature, without asking leave or depending upon the will of any other man" (p. 287). Despite the expansive terms in which Locke elaborates the potentialities of natural freedom (to order their actions, dispose of their possessions and persons), the condition is nevertheless a bounded one, limited by the obligations of natural law. Two paragraphs later, Locke explicitly states that, although the natural condition is one of freedom, it is not a "state of license" to do as one wishes (p. 288). Hence the puzzle: Locke insists on characterizing a condition in which he acknowledges human beings to be subject to obligations as one of perfect freedom.

To the extent that this puzzle can be resolved without complaining about Locke's use of terms, the resolution is the following. What Locke means by human beings being naturally free is that they are free in the specific sense in which Filmer denies freedom, namely, that they are free with respect to matters of political authority. The various obligations of natural law to which we are indeed obligated do not include an obligation with respect to the issue of political governance. As is well known, Locke makes political authority contingent on the consent of those over whom this authority is to be expressed. Thus, in contrast to Filmer, for whom scriptural authority prescribes, among other obligations, the particular form of political authority, for Locke we incur no such political obligations through either natural law or divine positive law.

The claim that natural freedom involves being free of any political obligations clarifies the contrast between Locke and Filmer. But without knowing what the obligations and limits of natural law are, one can scarcely give specific content to natural freedom. Without knowing the bounds within which we are obligated, we cannot know the specifically political sense in which we are free. Access to natural law, therefore, is an essential condition for realizing our natural freedom. It is here that the centrality of reason becomes evident. The human capacity to reason is the basis of our knowing the obligations of natural law and, by implication, the limits beyond which we are free of such obligations. In his *Reasonableness of Christianity*, Locke goes to great lengths to emphasize the basic congruity between the demands of natural law and the potentialities of human nature, specifically of human reason, to understand these laws: "God hath, by the light of reason, revealed to all mankind, *who would make use of that light*, that he was good and merciful. The same spark of the divine nature and knowledge in man, which making him a man, showed him the law he was under as a man."[2]

Such passages and several similar references in the *Two Treatises* underscore the importance of reason. But in all these instances, it is the capacity to reason that is natural, not its actual exercise. For example, in the first reference in the *Second Treatise* linking reason to natural law and to the state of nature as being governed by that law, Locke states: "The *state of nature* has a law to govern it, which obliges everyone: and reason, which is that law, teaches all mankind who will but consult it" (p. 289). Similarly, "the law of nature . . . [and] it is certain there is such a law,

---

[2] John Locke, *The Reasonableness of Christianity*, ed. I. T. Ramsey (Stanford: Stanford University Press, 1989), p. 55, emphasis added.

and that too, as intelligible and plain to a rational creature, and a studier of that law"[3] (p. 293). The use of the word "plain" in this citation can be misleading unless it is read, as the text presents it, in conjunction with the requirement that its plainness depend on the study of the law of nature. In the absence of such study, or when motivated by willfully perverse purposes, then—despite God's having implanted this capacity—we do not naturally have access to these laws.[4]

My purpose here is to draw out the close link between freedom, law, and reason. To the extent that being naturally free turns on knowing natural law and thus its limits, which in turn involves actualizing the capacity we have to reason, we are forced to acknowledge, as Locke acknowledges, the importance of education as the process through which the capacity to reason is actualized. Notwithstanding those who come to a knowledge of natural law through faith rather than reason, it appears that Locke still is committed to the view that freedom requires reason. Thus he says: "He that is not come to the use of his reason cannot be said to be *under this law*" and thus is not "presently free" (p. 323). Again, more concisely, "the *freedom* then of man and liberty of acting according to his own will, is *grounded on* his having *reason*" (p. 327). In terms of broad evidence from the *Second Treatise*, the point being made can be underscored by the fact that it is in the chapter "Paternal Power," in which Locke explicitly speaks of the duty of parents to educate their children,

[3] Apart from reason, there is another basis for access to natural law, and that is through faith. *In Reasonableness of Christianity*, Locke states, "The greatest part cannot know, and therefore they must believe" (p. 66). The precise status of this greatest part with respect to the doctrine of natural freedom and through it of consent to their political governors is a complex issue, which in the present context is beside my point. What is clear is that Locke closely links freedom with law and law with reason.

[4] There are as well those, like "lunaticks and ideots," in whom the capacity to reason is completely absent and who are therefore unambiguously excluded from the consensual politics of the *Second Treatise* (see pp. 325–26). See ibid., para. 60, p. 350.

that he, more than anywhere else, draws out the conception linking reason, freedom, and natural law.[5]

As with the chapter in the *Second Treatise*, where parental duties extend beyond merely training or actualizing the natural capacity to reason, the *Thoughts* is also a more comprehensive work in which the discussion of reason is part of a wider and more complex scheme for the education of young children. Indeed, it is clear that the process of reasoning cannot, in terms of what Locke says in the *Thoughts*, be distinguished from the comprehensive pedagogical schema. Within this problematic, my concern with the *Thoughts* is to look at this comprehensive pedagogical schema with a view to understanding the actualization of the capacity to reason, which is the linchpin between natural freedom and natural law.

Let me return to the other problematic that points to the importance of the *Thoughts* and Locke's views on education generally. At the broadest level, my purpose is to elaborate Locke's response to the cognitive considerations and attending anxieties referred to in the previous chapters. If the problem to which Locke is responding is not solely nor even primarily one in which individuals manifest a tendency to invade each other's turf and to be partial to themselves in the pursuit of their own interests, but rather one in which individuals display a lack of self-control and constancy, and as a result an episodic but nevertheless hazardous absence of moderation, then it is unlikely we can find these concerns addressed by focusing simply on Locke's political and institutional proposals. This is not to suggest that such proposals fall by the wayside or lose their pertinence, rather, their pertinence is acknowledged by reference to an alternative set of motives and considerations.

I have two goals in dealing with this particular problematic. The first is to make clear how Locke settles the mind of whose

[5] See especially sections 57–63 (pp. 323–27).

erratic excesses I have discussed in the previous chapter. Involved here is nothing less than the forging of individuality, an individuality that is, for the most part, presupposed within the naturalistic problematic but one, I suggest, that is the object of an extended and detailed constructive effort. The details of this effort occasion my second goal, which is to reveal how, while forging individuality, Locke simultaneously truncates its reach, its singularity, its independence and hence limits the likelihood of its being authentically free where the register of such freedom is not merely the actualized capacity to consent to political authority but rather must include, at a minimum, an acceptance of willful eccentricity. I take this to be a political claim. But it is where Locke identifies the problem, in the mind, that its resolution is manifested or becomes fully evident in what one might loosely call Locke's social and educational theory. Locke's educational writings on which I focus give us a particularly unguarded view of both the purposes that inform this chapter, the construction of individuality along with its simultaneous abridgement.[6] In making this claim, I am saying more than simply that education is important. This is true, and Locke is, perhaps more than any other modern writer, responsible for this claim having the overfamiliar and trite connotations it has. But further, the centrality of education is tied to a specific need to modify the natural self—a modification that can only be effected, as Locke repeatedly emphasizes, while the mind is compliant, supple, and unburdened by the effects of memory and reflection.

I noted in the previous chapter that the Lockean self, while exercising natural capacities, displays an anthropological potential that constantly threatens to extend beyond the bounds of

[6] Sheldon Wolin in his synthetic and original work *Politics and Vision*, points to the broad terms of this interpretation by suggesting how "the decline of political categories and the ascendancy of social ones are the distinguishing marks of our contemporary situation where political philosophy has been eclipsed by other forms of knowledge"; see p. 292 and also chap. 9.

political efficacy. Thus, his "busy mind" has to be cautioned against "meddling with things exceeding his comprehension." The creative potential of his imagination has to be disciplined and anchored by the "memory" of objects lest it effortlessly issue in a demented extravagance. In the use of words, he could not presume on "any natural connexion" with his ideas and certainly not between those words and the ideas they might excite in others (*Essay*, pp. 405, 408). In any case, his mind is subject to that peculiar unreasonableness in which "*ideas* that in themselves are not at all of kin, come to be so united in some Mens Minds, [such] that 'tis very hard to separate them" (p. 395). It is not surprising then that despite "Reason" being the "Law of Nature," a law that God has implanted in us, the Lockean self's natural freedom to order his actions and dispose of his possessions without asking leave of anyone has to be circumscribed by the textual qualification "within the bounds of the Law of Nature."

How should one interpret this and numerous similar qualifications from the *Two Treatises*? It could be taken as it is surely intended in one sense as an indication of the normative limits or borders within which we are free and beyond which we incur the preconventional obligations of the laws of nature. But it could also be read (without denying the former reading) as pointing to a fundamental and massive pedagogical project in which reason, for it to be "Reason" must, despite its divine origins, be "bound" and molded. This is just what Locke explicitly states in his chapter on paternal power in the *Second Treatise:* it is the duty of parents to educate their "nonage" until reason shall take their place. The implications of this latter reading suggest an alternative emphasis to that usually encountered within the naturalistic problematic. Although the capacity to reason is no doubt natural, reason—in the sense Locke deploys the term while portraying the state of nature and the conditions requisite for the commonwealth—is not only malleable but, in the absence of an appropriate mold, highly transgressive.

Two striking features underlie the examples I have recalled from the previous chapter. The first is that they refer to cognitive tendencies in the natural self and thus contrast with the common emphasis on interests and appetites. The second, closely related to the first, is that the significance of these examples is not assessed by virtue of the directed manner in which they violate another person's property or rights. Indeed, it is precisely the absence of design and direction that gives them, in Locke's view, their socially threatening potential. For instance, in the important chapter "Of the Association of Ideas" from the *Essay*, in which Locke discusses the madness that "so universally infects Mankind," his examples are conspicuously devoid of violent and politically deleterious effects. They involve musicians who can perform without regard to the notes, a man obsessed with eating honey such that the very mention of the word convulses his stomach into sickness, goblins and darkness. Yet, despite these apparently innocuous examples, Locke concludes his discussion of the association of ideas and madness with the claim that it is the "foundation of the most dangerous . . . error in the world" (p. 401).

These cognitive failings do have enormous social consequences for Locke, but these consequences do not stem from the poignancy of the other-regarding motive that might be concealed behind their effects. Instead, it is the absence of any motive, the sheer randomness and lack of control they evince, that gives them, in Locke's view, their socially grave potential. And this again suggests the distortions and misplaced emphasis involved in thinking of Locke as concerned solely or primarily with the basis and limits on political authority.

The picture emerging from these examples is not that of an individual well possessed of natural capacities, and through them of interests, and involved in the singular pursuit of appetites; rather, it that is of an underdeveloped individuality without internal moorings, habits, or direction--almost possessed by natural capacities that are not fully fathomed or controlled. Such a person is in need of distinction, of a mold that will supply individuality.

When one accepts the foundational assumptions of freedom, rationality, and equality as defining the individuality of the Lockean self who now requires only political society to ensure peace and order, one overlooks the depth and acuity of this need. For Locke as for liberalism, individuality is an aspiration, a process of coming-to-be, and not a foundational given that liberal political institutions are merely designed to regulate and secure. To understand and judge liberalism simply by reference to the political and juridical constraints it places on individuals in the course of regulating and securing their individuality is to overlook the constructive agenda, also a part of liberalism, through which this individuality is fashioned in the first place. The picture of liberalism as an ideology and ethic of sobriety and activism, of individual and collective security, and of individual rights and governmental restraint may be, as such summaries go, an adequate one. But, notwithstanding this appealing gloss, it does not vitiate the claim that it approaches this settlement by responding to a deep anxiety regarding the libertine excesses to which human beings are naturally prone. Once one acknowledges this possibility, it becomes imperative to consider the various and not merely political processes through which this settlement is achieved.

Education and the Malleability of the Mind

That human malleability and education are the most decisive factors in the process of forming the mind is conspicuous from the outset of Locke's *Thoughts Concerning Education*. His repeated emphasis of both points makes the relative neglect this work has received puzzling even beyond what it in any case would be on the basis of its conceptual centrality. Locke opens the *Thoughts*, having already in the epistle said that "errors in education should be less indulged than any: these like faults in the first concoction, that are never mended in the second or third, carry their after-wards-incorrigible taint with them," with the following:

> I think I may say, that of all the men we meet with, nine parts out of ten are what they are, good or evil, useful or not, by their education. 'Tis that which makes the great difference in man-kind. The little and almost insensible impressions on our ten-der infancies, have very important and lasting consequences: and there 'tis, as in the fountains of some rivers, where a gentle application of the hand turns the flexible waters into channels, that make them take quite contrary courses, and by this little direction given them at first in the source, they receive dif-ferent tendencies, and arrive at last at very remote and distant places. (p. 112)

> I imagine the minds of children as easily turned this or that way as water itself. (Pp. 114–15)

I quote at length both because of what Locke says and the way he says it. In a work in which the emphasis on religious and scrip-tural training is singularly limited, it is surely striking if not blasphemous for Locke to make good and evil so heavily depen-dent on education. Similarly, even if one relegates as only appro-priate to a later interpretive fashion and freedom the implications of alluding to the "almost insensible impressions on our tender infancies" along with the sexually evocative imagery of education as "the hand [that] turns the flexible waters into channels," Locke's language is still surely striking. The use of the river metaphor even more than the blank slate, white paper, and wax tablet imagery of the *Essay* suggests an acute need for early intervention in the absence of which the effects on the mind are dire and incorrigible. The reference to these effects as decisive even when the impressions are still insensible, particularly given the absence of an elaborate theory of early infant development, seems only to emphasize the point that the effects of education go all the way down. Whereas the malleability of children's minds are akin to water, their bodies are "clay cottages" and hence similarly in need of parental molding and thus "not to be neglected" (p. 115).[7]

What the above passage does not make fully evident, even though it is in a sense the most vivid feature of the *Thoughts*, is how the challenge of education becomes a detailed and mundane preoccupation with the minute particulars of everyday existence. Although the work was arguably the most influential source for changes in British childrearing practices and education more generally all through the eighteenth century, its influence did not stem from any announced abstract principles.[8] In a letter to Edward Clarke, Locke says that "there are a thousand other things that need consideration" (p. 363). Even a cursory reading of the *Thoughts* makes clear the range of issues and the detail with which parental guidance had to concern itself. The work ranges over a concern with toilet training; the type of bed (quilted rather than feathered); the appropriate foods to be consumed at various times; the imprudence of wearing shaped and tight-fitting bodices; the importance of knowing how to dance, fence, and ride; the appropriate comportment toward servants and others of lower rank; and the significance of being able to feign humility, anger, and concern. It is not surprising that the work was employed as a veritable manual by generations of European parents. The significance of this feature of the *Thoughts* is that it under-

---

[7] Locke emphasizes this point when he says, "I do not doubt but it is, *viz.* that the difference to be found in the manners and abilities of men, is owing more to their *education* than to anything else" (pp. 137–38), and again in his references to the minds of children as being akin to soil in which one can plant various seeds but must also be attentive to the weeds that can spoil them (pp. 158, 160).

[8] See James Axtell's critical and editorial commentary, *Thoughts*, pp. 3–105.

scores the importance of contextual particulars as decisive to, not only issues of breeding, class affiliation, and what goes under the general heading of character development, but also the determination of good or evil, reasoning, and, most important, what it means to be free.

An emphasis on contextual details also gives concrete credence to Locke's critique of innate ideas and principles in the *Essay*. In challenging the dispositional and innatist orthodoxy represented by figures such as the Cambridge Platonist Ralph Cudworth, Lord Herbert of Cherbury, Leibniz, and Henry Lee, Locke not only asserts the falsity of these ideas but claims instead that custom and education are the main grounds on which propositions are assented to. Instead of viewing assent as dependent on a natural disposition to the truth, Locke divests the mind of any such telic faculty and instead makes speculative and moral principles dependent wholly on constructed and conventionally habituated grounds.[9] The *Thoughts*, along with the *Conduct of the Understanding*, which was originally intended as the longest chapter of the *Essay*, can be thought of as filling out an assertion from Book II of the *Essay*:

> Custom settles habits of thinking in the understanding, as well as of determining the will, and of motions in the body; all of which seems to be but trains of motion in the animal spirits, which once set agoing continue on in the same steps they have been used to, which by often treading are worn into a smooth path, and the motion in it becomes easy and as it were natural. (P. 396)

---

[9] See, for example, *Essay*, pp. 83, 101. The standard account of the numerous philosophical and historical issues involved in this debate is John Yolton's *John Locke and the Way of Ideas* (Oxford: Oxford University Press, 1956). James Tully in "Governing Conduct," offers an excellent summary of the historical and philosophical stakes of Locke's critique, along with a provocative interpretation that emphasizes probabilistic considerations in the governing of assent.

In effect, customs and habits settle and define the form individuality takes.

The *Thoughts* is the sort of work that cannot be summarized. It lacks an argumentary order and a clear synthetic structure. What follows is an attempt to cull from it three persistent preoccupations or themes which, although they do not capture the range of this work, bear on the issue of individuality and supply an obvious synaptic link with Locke's more familiar political proposals from the *Second Treatise*. They can also be seen as a direct response to the cognitive and subjective anxieties that characterize the natural self discussed in the previous chapter. The themes are (a) self-restraint and submission (b) the privatization of publicity and (c) the inculcation of distinctions and social self-discipline.

I exclude as a distinct theme Locke's previously referred to emphasis on habits as the principle mode of conditioning human behavior. This exclusion is not meant to suggest a limited importance. Locke's assertion of habituation as fundamental and primary is undeniable. But the emphasis on habits in itself leaves the range of possible alternatives wide open. One could, for instance, be habituated into having an extravagant imagination or displaying a singular lack of self-restraint. Locke does not as a rule associate habituation per se with salutary effects. After all, it is the wrong and dangerous "connection in our mind" that is of "so great [a] force to set us awry in our actions," and these early habits can overturn all morality (*Essay*, p. 397). The emphasis on habits is thus not linked to a substantively specific pedagogical project. There is, however, one aspect of habits as a means of molding the individual which singles it out as especially important. Locke's principal though not exclusive concern in the *Thoughts* is with very young children. On numerous occasions he makes comments such as the following: "Those therefore that intend to ever govern their children should begin it whilst they are *very little*"; "If you would have him [the child] stand in awe of you, imprint it *in his infancy*"; "Children (earlier perhaps than we think) are very sensible to *praise* and commendation" (pp. 145, 153). The emphasis on habituation combined with this focus on very young children has the effect of making whatever is habituated *appear* natural. Thus, "bowing to a gentleman when he salutes him [the child], and looking in his face when he speaks to him, is by constant use as natural to a well-bred man, as breathing; it requires no thought, no reflection." As well, "this will beget habits in them, which, being once established, operate of themselves easily and naturally, without the assistance of the memory" (pp. 157, 158). This suggests two points of importance. First, the effects of education cannot be left to the vagaries of thought, reflection, and the recollection of rules; this implies the second point, that Locke's pedagogical interventions are literally directed at the construction of human nature or, at any rate, of something that could not readily be distinguished from human nature.

The purpose of the stated themes is to suggest the particular traits Locke wants habituated, and hence the particular response he offers to the subjectivity of the self. It is only by understanding the details of Locke's constructive project that one arrives at an appreciation of the extent of the transformations on the natural self. It is these details that constitute the habits that are "woven into the very principles of his [the child's] nature" (p. 138) and thus presumed in the contractual agreements he makes in entering the commonwealth.

Self-Restraint and Submission

In his famous study *The Protestant Ethic and the Spirit of Capitalism*, Max Weber emphasized the links between Calvinism and the rise of modern capitalism, and the concomitant dominance of rationalization as a political, social, and economic tendency and practice. Calvinism, in his view,

> attempted to subject man to the supremacy of a purposeful will, to bring his actions under constant self-control with a careful consideration of their ethical consequences. This active self-control . . . was also the most important practical ideal of Puritanism. . . . The Puritan, like every rational type of asceticism, tried to enable a man to maintain and act upon his constant motives, especially those which it taught him itself, against the emotions. In this formal psychological sense of the term, it tried to make him into a personality.[10]

Among the many senses in which Weber's study was profound and original, one was the claim that a commitment to a particular set of ideas led to a psychological transformation in the individual and hence the construction of a particular personality. My interpretation of Locke derives from Weber in the sense that I am also concerned with how a particular personality was constructed. The sense in which this interpretation deviates from, although in no sense does it contradict, Weber's view is in emphasizing not a particular set of ideas or beliefs but rather a particular view of the natural tendency of the mind as the antecedent basis to the construction of a particular personality.

Weber's thesis was taken up by the great German historian Otto Hintze to explore the links between Calvinism and the rise of the modern state, and along with it the rise of the ideology of raison d'etat. As with Weber, Hintze's interpretation placed great emphasis on the importance of self-control in effecting these transformations.[11] Numerous more recent studies of Cal-

---

[10] Max Weber, *The Protestant Ethic and the Spirit of Capitalism*, trans. Talcott Parsons (New York: Charles Scribners Sons, 1958), p. 119.

[11] Otto Hintze, "Calvinism and Raison d'Etat in Early Seventeenth Century Brandenburg," in *The Historical Essays of Otto Hintze*, ed. F. Gilbert (New York: Oxford University Press, 1975), pp. 88–154.

vinism, Puritanism, and the sixteenth and seventeenth centuries more generally have rightly focused on the importance of self-control as a theological commitment of the ideas in this period.[12] They also feature the Protestant and especially Puritan conceptions of duty, self-denial, and calling.

It is not surprising that these ideas have facilitated our understanding of Locke. Both biographically and intellectually, Locke belongs within the general embrace of such Protestant convictions. The *Thoughts* in particular is replete with the resonance of familiar Puritan injunctions. Thus, at the outset he states that "the great principle and foundation of all virtue and worth, is placed in this, that a man may be able to *deny himself* his own desires, cross his own inclinations and purely follow what reason directs as best, tho' the appetites lean the other way" (p. 138). Only a few paragraphs later, he repeats himself using almost exactly the same words (p. 143). Later he states that "to make a good, a wise, and a virtuous man 'tis fit he should learn to cross his appetite, and deny his inclination to *riches, finery, or pleasing his palate*, &c" (p. 151). This emphasis on self-denial has its corollary in a corresponding emphasis in the importance of self-mastery:

> It is of great moment, and worth our endeavors, to teach the mind to get the mastery over itself; and to be able, upon choice, to take itself off from the hot pursuit of one thing, and set itself upon another with facility and delight; or at any time to shake off its sluggishness, and vigorously employ itself about what reason or the advice of another shall direct. (Pp. 174-75)

[12] Walzer, *Revolution of the Saints;* Sacvan Bercovich, *The Puritan Origins of the American Self* (New Haven: Yale University Press, 1975); Johan Huizinga, *The Waning of the Middle Ages* (Garden City: Doubleday, 1954); Dunn, *Political Thought of John Locke;* William Paden, "Theaters of Humility and Suspicion: Desert Saints and New England Puritans," in *Technologies of the Self,* ed. Luther H. Martin, Huck Gutman, and Patrick H. Hutton (Amherst: University of Massachusetts Press, 1988), pp. 64-79.

It seems to me that two questions follow from this evident and copious identification with self-denial and self-restraint:[13] In response to what exigency is this emphasis to be understood? What precisely is involved in achieving the self-restraint Locke enjoins? Michael Walzer in *The Revolution of the Saints* can be understood by virtue of his emphasis on Puritan ideas to respond to the first question by suggesting that the emphasis on self-control is a constitutive idea of Puritan ethical values. In this, he is at least partially following the lead of Weber, who also starts his study with the consideration of Puritan ideas. A similar response that focuses on the theological basis of this emphasis is evident in Sacvan Bercovich's reading of Puritan, particularly early American, texts.[14] E. P. Thompson and C. B. Macpherson transform the first question by responding to it as less a concern with self-control than a concern with discipline; they see it as a reaction to the growing exigencies of emerging industrial capitalism.[15]

Regarding the second question, Weber's response is no doubt the most famous and for my purposes the most relevant. Having identified an abiding commitment to Calvinist ideas and especially these ideas as they pertain to the issue of salvation and the uncertainty of grace, Weber claimed that the fear deriving from this commitment engendered a psychological transformation and induced self-discipline. As an aside, one might point to a contrast between Weber's understanding and Hobbes's of the capacity of awe and terror to tame or discipline certain passions,

---

[13] See sections 33, 36, 38, 39, 40, 46, 52, 70, 75, 78 in the *Thoughts*, pp. 138–79.

[14] Bercovich, *Puritan Origin*. Also see Edmund Leites, *The Puritan Conscience and Modern Sexuality* (New Haven: Yale University Press, 1986), especially pp. 34–50.

[15] E. P. Thompson, "Time, Work-Discipline and Industrial Capitalism," *Past and Present* 38 (December 1967), 56–97; C. B. Macpherson, *The Political Theory of Possessive Individualism* (Oxford: Oxford University Press, 1962). Also see E. J. Hundert, "The Making of Homo-Faber: John Locke between Ideology and History," *Journal of the History of Ideas* 33, no. 1 (1972), 3–22.

particularly pride.[16] Unlike Weber, for Hobbes as for Madison there is no psychic change, simply a counteracting of one passion (pride) by another (fear).

In his understudied *Neostoicism and the Early Modern State*, Gerhard Oestreich offers what can be taken as a sympathetic correction of Weber. Instead of focusing on Calvinist theology and its preoccupation with salvation, Oestreich considers the widespread revival from the mid-sixteenth century of Stoic themes and values. The revival of Roman political values such as *auctoritas, temperantia, constantia,* and *disciplina* is linked to the rise of the modern state and seen as a response to the need for widespread social discipline: "Bureaucracy, militarism, and mercantilism were all manifestations of social discipline in particular spheres, different ways of serving the state." Oestreich further links this need for social discipline with a ubiquitous concern with passions: "Contemplating the seventeenth century picture of man—in religious terms a prey to sin, in philosophic terms a victim of his passions—one begins to appreciate the extent of the preoccupation with discipline."[17] Weber's concept of rationalization is not, in Oestreich's view, broad enough to capture the multifarious implications of this foundational preoccupation with the passions and their implications not only for the major political and social institutions of the state but also for more distant considerations such as town planning.[18]

It is precisely this preoccupation with the passions and particularly cognitive passions that I have been pressing in this

[16] Hobbes, *Leviathan*, pp. 337–55.

[17] Gerhard Oestreich, *Neostoicism and the Early Modern State*, ed. Brigitta Oestreich and H. G. Koenigsberger, trans. David McLintock (Cambridge: Cambridge University Press, 1982), pp. 268–69.

[18] "Man was disciplined with regard to his desires and the way he expressed himself. He sought to attain self-control, which was the highest goal. He disciplined nature too, with artistically clipped trees and hedges of seventeenth century parks and gardens. The same process found expression in the police ordinances of the towns, the territories, and the Empire"; ibid., pp. 269–70.

work, and it is the passions which I believe underlie Locke's concern with self-discipline and self-mastery. I turn therefore to the second question, namely, what is involved in achieving self-restraint and self-mastery? It is tempting to think that Locke's answer is an elaborate scheme of habituation—that is, that his response to a situation in which human beings manifest a natural tendency to be subject to passions they do not fully control is to habituate in them certain temperate responses that would, as it were, help counteract this tendency. This suggestion is at best only partially true, for although it is the case, as I have mentioned, that Locke proposes "repeating the same action 'til it be grown habitual in them [and hence] the performance will not depend on memory or reflection" (*Thoughts*, p. 157), he is in fact substantively much more specific about what this habituation must achieve. Consider the first of Locke's innumerable and extensive references to self-discipline:

> We are generally wise enough to begin with them, when they are *very young;* and discipline *betimes* [at an early time] those other creatures we would make useful and good for somewhat. They are only our own offspring, that we neglect on this point; and having made them ill children, we foolishly expect they should be good men. . . . They [grapes and sugar-plums] are objects as suitable to the longing of one of more years, as what he cried for when little, was to the inclinations of a child. The having of desires accommodated to the apprehensions and relish of those several ages is not the fault; but the not having them subject to the rules and constraints of Reason: the difference lies not in the having or not having of appetites, but in the power to govern, and deny ourselves in them. He that is not used to submit his will to the reason of others, when he is young, will scarce harken or submit to his own reason, when he is of an age to make use of it. (Pp. 139–40)

There are two main themes in this passage, submission and self-discipline. The first reference to the former resonates with a common formulation from the *Second Treatise* in which what it means to be free is to act in conformity with the dictates of reason, which itself is allied with the laws of nature. Hence, one might say, freedom involves acting under the discipline of one's reason. In this passage, the desires are to be constrained by reason. The desires that are thus constrained, we are led to believe, define what is meant by self-discipline. The intuitive idea, one might think, is that self-discipline requires acting in such a way such that one is literally disciplined and that this disciplining derives from the authority of one's own reason. But this interpretation turns out, in view of the last sentence of the passage, to be only partially what Locke has in mind. For here it becomes apparent that self-discipline requires submission not to one's own reason but rather to the reason of others. The experience of submission to others is thus a necessary precondition for being able to submit to one's own reason, and hence a precondition for self-discipline.

This claim elaborates the idea put forth in the *Second Treatise* that it is the duty of parents to guide their children until reason can take their place, at which point the children have the requisite conditions for being free (pp. 324–30). But what becomes clear from the passages just quoted and what is only hinted at in the *Second Treatise* is that this requisite condition is not mere guidance but rather the specific experience of submission to authority. The importance of parental nurture from the standpoint of realizing one's capacity for freedom, rationality, and self-discipline is not that parents supply the essential conditions for the survival and the early well-being of a child. Rather, their essential link with the child's future freedom, rationality, and self-discipline is that these attributes require as a necessary precondition an early molding of the will that can occur only through the experience of submission to one's parents and guardians. Locke is emphatic on this point. The unruly passions and tendencies of a young child's mind require the experience of submission to others before they can be guided by the child's own reason:[19] "The *younger* they are, the less I think are their unruly and disorderly appetites to be complied with; and the less reason they have of their own, the more they are to be under the absolute power and restraint of those, in whose hands they are." He continues in the following paragraph: "Those therefore that intend ever to govern their children should begin it whilst they are *very little;* and look that they perfectly comply with the will of their parents. . . . Be sure then to establish the authority of a father, *as soon* as he [the child] is capable of submission, and can understand in whose power he is." And again: "For, methinks, they mightily misplace the treatment due to their children, who are indulgent and familiar, when they are little. For, liberty and indulgence can do no good to *children:* Their want of judgment makes them stand in need of restraint and discipline" (pp. 144–45).

There is, for Locke, a clear tripartite relationship between the exercise of parental authority, the inculcation of reason and judgment in the child, and the realization of the capacity for self-restraint, again in the child. Thus the crucial capacity for reason, which is the basis for being free and for abiding by the laws of nature, and which in the *Second Treatise* is presented as a natural capacity, itself requires parental molding of the will, which in turn requires the experience of early submission to parental authority. Locke does not draw out the links I am suggesting in an explicit and schematic manner. But they are, I believe, all but explicit in the two following extended passages from the *Thoughts:*

> I imagine every one will judge it reasonable, that their children, when little, should look upon their parents as their lords, their absolute governors and that, when they come to riper

---

[19] All the passages I draw from in this section come from that portion of the *Thoughts* in which Locke is expressly dealing with the mind. Locke is concerned with the body in the first thirty-three sectors.

years, they should look on them as their best, as their only sure
friends. The way I have mentioned, if I mistake not, is the
only one to obtain this. We should look upon our children,
when grown up, to be like ourselves; with the same passions,
the same desires. We would be thought rational creatures and
have our freedom; we love not to be uneasie under constant
rebukes. Whoever has such treatment when he is a man, will
look out other company, other friends, other conversation,
with whom he can be at ease. If therefore a strict hand be kept
over children *from the beginning*, they will in that age be tract-
able and quietly submit to it, as never having known any other:
and if, as they grow up to the use of reason, the rigor of
government be, as they deserve it, gently relaxed, the father's
brow more smooth'd to them, and the distance by degrees
abated; his former restraints will increase their love, when
they find it was only a kindness to them, and a care to make
them capable to deserve the favor of their parents, and the
esteem of everybody else. (P. 146)

He that has not a mastery over his inclinations, he that knows
not how to *resist* the importunity of *present pleasure or pain*, for
the sake of what reason tells him is fit to be done, wants the true
principle of virtue and industry; and is in danger never to be
good for anything. This temper therefore, so contrary to un-
guided nature, is to be got betimes; and this habit, as the true
foundation of future ability and happiness, is to be wrought
into the mind, as early as may be, even from the first dawnings
of any knowledge, or apprehension in children; and so to be
confirmed in them, by all the care and ways imaginable, by
those who have the over-sight of their education. (P. 148)

Clearly, reason, self-discipline, and virtue are the products of an
early immersion in the disciplinary and hierarchical matrix of
the family. Whatever the natural capacities in the child, there is
neither the assurance nor even the likelihood that, in the absence
of this matrix, they would be actualized to take the form of

reason, self-discipline, and virtue. In reviving the Stoic emphasis on self-denial and self-mastery, Locke nevertheless puts a wholly distinct twist on it. For the Stoics, *askesis* is an amalgam of renunciation, self-examination, and withdrawal from the world as preparation for access into a higher reality. It therefore involves *gymnasia*, literally "to train oneself" in artificially induced exercises of physical hardship and privation, sexual abstinence, and rituals of purification and concentration. All these exercises resonate with Locke's proposals for the education of young children, but with an important difference. They have lost the solitary tonality evident in Lucretius' *De Rerum Naturae* or in the significance Marcus Aurelius' country home has for him as a spiritual retreat from the town.[20] Instead, for Locke these exertions are now part of an orchestrated social environment of domestic space, suffused with the minutiae of parental incentives and strictures and already informed by structures of authority.

The Privatization of Public Standards

In the history of educational theory and reform, Locke has rightly been credited with introducing and popularizing a change to a more benign and liberal regime.[21] In support of this, one might offer his emphasis on the importance of physical health; his de-emphasis of the method of rote memorization, of stuffing the child's mind with rules of grammar, morality, courtesy, and

---

[20] See M. Foucault, "Technologies of the Self," in *Technologies of the Self*, ed. Martin, Gutman, and Hutton, pp. 16–49.

[21] See James Axtell, "The 'Education' in Context," and "Locke and Scientific Education," in *Thoughts*, pp. 49–87; Tarcov, *Locke's Education for Liberty*. Also see Peter Gay's introduction to *John Locke on Education*, ed. Peter Gay (New York: Columbia University, Bureau of Publications, Teacher's College, 1964), and Francis W. Garforth's introduction to Locke's, *Conduct of the Understanding*.

conduct; his accommodation of the need for amusement and measured frivolousness; his emphasis on tailoring pedagogy to the temperament and age of children; his acknowledgment of girls as worthy of focused parental concern; his mocking and acerbic remarks on the stifling overemphasis of Latin and Greek; and, most important, his extended diatribe against corporal punishment or, as he says, the rule of the rod. There is no question that the *Thoughts* is a work rich with the spirit of an enlightened rationalism in which, whatever his larger purpose, considerations of freedom and reason are conspicuous.

The positive assessment commonly attached to these changes is, no doubt, linked to our own contemporary attitudes about education. His reforms offer a clear and convenient historical realignment that can be seen as culminating in many current educational ideas. [22] It is not my purpose to either challenge this self-referential basis of judging Locke or, in any extended manner, to take issue with assessments of Locke's specific proposals. Instead, I want to introduce an element of skepticism by pointing to features which, if seen, as laudatory precursors of our own ideas, should involve us in embarrassing self-assessment.

In the previous section, I indicated how self-restraint is inextricably and fundamentally linked with authoritarian aspects of the patriarchal family and thus implicates what appears as an individual virtue with obvious importance for an individualistic politics. In the present section, I extend the broad terms of this interpretation by noting how Locke's ostensibly liberal and compassionate program is counterbalanced by the demand that the child internalize the standards—the anguishing standards—of shame, guilt, and responsibility. The meanings of these terms all depend on a complex system of public or social valuation—even

---

[22] See Amy Gutman, *Democratic Education* (Princeton: Princeton University Press, 1987). See also Tarcov, *Locke's Education for Liberty*, and Frank Carlton, *Economic Influences upon Educational Progress in the United States, 1820–1850* (New York: Teacher's College Press, 1966).

when, as in the case of guilt, the ultimate significance of the term derives from a theological narrative. The internalization of these standards thus involves the internalization of this system of valuation. For Locke, the displacement of the rule of the rod is linked with the counterproductive and inefficient way this rule propagates the adherence to public standards. Corporal punishment is a brutal response to transgression which effects its power directly on the tactile surface of the transgressor—the body. In this, it manifests a strange timidity by not acknowledging the real power of the parent, which is over the malleable contours of the child's mind. It is the almost infinite efficacy of this latter power that Locke wishes to animate and propagate.

Locke often runs together two critical ideas. The first, to which sufficient reference has been made in the previous section, is that a child's mind is malleable, compliant, supple; and the second is that, to settle the direction of this mind, parents should literally inform it with public standards. Here one sees what Foucault has forcefully pointed to in the context of penal incarceration, the administration of madness, and more generally the science of man, namely, how a particular form of knowledge—in this case, regarding the malleability of the mind—comes to support a novel form of power. It is the extent of Locke's commitment to the second idea which, in my view, ultimately vitiates the possibility of a self-consciously willful and robust individuality emerging from it, and which once again shows how the naturalistic problematic that presumes freedom and rationality eclipses Locke's own truncation of these capacities.

On the face of it, Locke's objections to corporal punishment are straightforward and familiar. Such punishment does not root out the source of the infractions that make it necessary. Instead, it supplies greater reason for these infractions by encouraging a child to "dissemble obedience, whilst the fear of the rod hangs over him; but when that is removed, and by being out of sight, he can promise himself impunity, he [thus] gives greater scope to his natural inclination; which by this way [that is, by beating] is not at all altered, but on the contrary heightened and increased in him." The same reason leads Locke to strongly object to the use of rewards as inducements to perform the desired behavior: "When you promise him a *lace-cravat*, or a *fine new suit*, upon the performance of some of his little tasks; what do you by proposing these *rewards*, but allow them to be the good things he should aim at and thereby encourages longing for them, and accustom him to place his happiness in them." Such inducements do not accustom children to "submit to reason" (pp. 150–51).

It is not that Locke is wholly opposed either to punishment or to the inducement of rewards. Rather, it is that punishments and rewards are generally ill-chosen. They effect the "pains and pleasures of the body" and are not therefore directed at the principle of virtue which requires self-denial dependent on the intervention of the mind. Hence, a change in the object at which punishment and reward are directed is required: "Til you bring him to be able to bear a denial of that satisfaction, the child may at present be quiet and orderly but the disease is not cured." It is on this that Locke focuses his attention: "*Esteem* and *disgrace* are, of all others, the most powerful incentives to the mind. . . . If you can once get into children a love of credit, and an apprehension of shame and disgrace, you have put into them the true principle, which will constantly work, and incline them to the right" (pp. 152–53).

Locke gives two reasons for this endorsement of esteem and disgrace over the rod. The first is that children are ("earlier perhaps than we think") particularly sensitive to praise, commendation, and its denial. The effects of such rewards are "more than threats or blows, which lose their force" (p. 153). The second reason is presented as instrumental from the standpoint of the child, but in the process it also reveals Locke's own instrumentality. Esteem and disgrace indicate to children standards by which to assess who is doing well, who is disgraced, who is "beloved and cherished by everybody," and who on the other side is the object of contempt and "dis-esteem" (p. 154). The early inculcation of this rationality, of this reputational calculus, improves the child's own future prospects. Locke now reverts to speaking to the parents: "If by these means you [the parents] can come once to shame them out of their faults, (for besides that, I would willingly have no punishment) and make them in love with the pleasure of being well thought on, you may turn them as you please, and they will be in love with all the ways of virtue" (p. 154). Here again we have a tripartite connection between the effectiveness of shame, the power of parents to mold their children ("you may turn them as you please"), and the implied guarantee that children will stay on the path of virtue. The link between the first and third of these terms is striking, for it makes clear that virtue itself involves the acknowledgement of reputation and presumably other social and conventional markings. No mention is made of virtue requiring self-denial and the crossing of inclinations, as when Locke first speaks of the principle of virtue. Instead, the assurance of virtue is implied by the rationality shame and reputation induce, that is, the "love with the pleasure of being well thought on." Locke all but acknowledges this affiliation between virtue and reputation:

> Concerning reputation, I shall only remark this one thing more of it; that 'tho it be not the true principle and measure of virtue, (for that is the Knowledge of a man's duty, and the satisfaction it is to obey his Maker, in following the dictates of that light God has given him) yet it is that, which comes nearest to it: And being the testimony and applause that *other people's reason, as it were by a common consent,* give to virtuous and well-ordered actions, it is the proper guide and encouragement to children, 'til they grow able to judge for themselves, and find what is right by their own reason. (P. 156)

What a remarkable parenthesis. It reveals our ultimate duty to our maker only to displace it with the quotidian concern with the testimony and applause of other people's reason. A century later, a Bentham would altogether dispense with such a parenthetical nod. But Locke must acknowledge the true principle of virtue even while he points to its similitude with a crass reputational calculus. It is as though the Christian in Locke is obligated to flag his own apostasy by simultaneously pointing to his former and present self. And, as if to clear all incriminating traces of this enormous transvaluation in the principle of virtue, Locke wants it instilled in children before they have the reflection and memory to recall its intrusion. Of course, it might be claimed that Locke ends this passage with the suggestion that conforming to other people's reason and common consent is only a supporting precondition for when they exercise their own, perhaps singularly eccentric, reason. But this is hardly a credible possibility given the nature and extent of the socialization and the fact that, in any case, reputation bears the closest resemblance to the principle of virtue. Deviation and singularity of behavior from these standards of common consent may still be possible, but it will, for Locke, manifest both a failure of parental guidance and, more important, a straying from the principle of virtue.

Immediately after advising parents about the incentives of esteem and disgrace, Locke considers the difficulty involved in instilling this register of self-assessment in children: "The great difficulty here, is, I imagine, from the folly and perverseness of servants. . . . Children discountenanced by their parents for any fault, find usually a refuge and relief in the caresses of those foolish flatterers, who thereby undo whatever the parents endeavor to establish" (pp. 154, 164). Locke's many references to servants and "others of lower rank" consistently carry this double reproach—first, that they constitute a serious threat to the correct education of children, and second, that they have this effect because they shower the child with an excessive warmth and affection.[23] They are thus the purveyors of indiscretion who

[23] See *Thoughts*, sections 59, 67, 69, 70, 71 (pp. 154–72). With reference to the issue of esteem and disgrace, Locke's extended discussions of the importance of

indiscriminately valorize people and situations—and thus on Locke's reckoning threaten to undermine the correct assessment of the reputational calculus, the principle of virtue, which the child is meant to imbibe. The refuge and relief offered by servants is clearly not the esteem Locke wishes for them to understand and appreciate.

There is one remarkable exception to Locke's compassionate injunctions against corporal punishment. For children who fall within the reach of this exception, Locke not only permits the rule of the rod but encourages it with brutal and enthusiastic gusto: "*Stubbornness*, and an *obstinate disobedience*, must be master'd with force and blows: for this there is no other remedy. Whatever particular action you bid him do, or forbear, you must be sure to see yourself obey'd; no quarter [i.e., clemency] in this case, no resistance" (p. 177). Locke offers a single reason for this exception: those who are stubborn and obstinate manifest this behavior by virtue of a willful resistance that has its roots in a perverse independence of *mind*. This independence blocks the authority of parents and thus denies the essential premise on which the *Thoughts* is based, that an infant's mind is malleable and hence receptive to the modifications of parental authority. Stubbornness and obstinacy, by challenging this premise, must be broken until the effects of the rod are, as it were, literally felt on the surface of the mind. Consider the example Locke gives to corroborate his point:

> A prudent and kind mother, of my acquaintance, was, on such an occasion, forced to whip her little daughter, at her first coming home from Nurse, eight times successively the same morning, before she could master her *stubbornness*, and obtain a compliance in a very easy and indifferent matter. If she had left off sooner, and stopped at the seventh whipping, she had spoilt

---

appropriate company and the choice of a tutor are revealing; see sections 66, 68–72, 88–94.

> the child forever; and, by her unprevailing blows, only con-
> firmed her *refractoriness*, very hardly afterwards to be cured;
> but wisely persisting, 'til she had bent her mind, and suppled
> her will, the only end of correction and chastisement, she
> established her authority thoroughly in the first occasion, and
> had ever after a very ready compliance and obedience in all
> things from her daughter. (P. 178)

This little girl represents the limiting point of Locke's compas-
sion. She is, one must assume, less than three years old. Her
mother is kind, but clearly more prudent, for she perceives in her
little daughter the threat she poses to an entire edifice of authority
and social relations. One can only guess what gesture of her little
body revealed her mind's refractoriness, what particular shrill-
ness of the screech, following the eighth whip, now made clear
her compliant will and her "bent" mind. Again, one can only
wonder why, in one of the very few examples in the *Thoughts* of a
mother and her daughter, the latter should serve as a metonomy
for a form of defiant alterity in the face of which liberalism
deploys the weapons of absolutism, brandished by the mother
with a horrifying but precisely calibrated tenacity and certainty.

Distinctions: A Sense of Self and One's Place in the World

In the chapter "Of Property" in the *Second Treatise*, Locke ex-
plains and justifies how the world that was given to humankind
in common was parceled into privately held units. His argument
turns on individual human labor being the principal source of
what makes the world valuable. It is the infusion of this labor
into a commonly held but nevertheless intrinsically valueless
world that entitles individuals to have a private right to the
portions on which they have labored and to which they have
added value (pp. 314–17). It is also this process and the distinct
claims that derive from it which establish a distinction among

individuals: "And 'tis plain, if the first gathering made them [acorns, apples, etc.] not his, nothing else could. That *labor* put a distinction between them and [the] common. That added something to them more than nature, the common mother of all, had done; and so they became his private right" (p. 306). This passage expresses the idea that a person's distinct humanity is manifest through the capacity for purposeful labor through which he or she acquires a public standing.[24] This person's property becomes, as it were, a public signature, a mark of uniqueness, of freedom, of rationality, and even of equality with others to the extent that they similarly impress themselves on the world. The idea of labor as a kind of unique signature is underscored by Locke's numerous references to the body, its various limbs, and hence to the distinctness of the individual of whom they are a part: "The labor of his body, the work of his hands we may say are properly his" (pp. 305–6), To the extent that property comes to be thus associated with the creativity, dignity, and distinctness of human beings, one can understand how Locke, in summarizing his own political ideas as nothing more than protection of property, can be seen as defending a larger, more noble enterprise (pp. 373–74).

In the present section I briefly extend the analysis of the previous two sections and suggest an alternative conception of the individuality of human beings. Here, as in the previous sections, my purpose is to reveal how Locke's conception of human individuality is, from its outset (i.e., from childhood), compromised by the dual emphasis on indicating the conditions for its possibility and simultaneously limiting its acceptable form. And here again the acceptable and its unacceptable obverse are distinguished by reference to what settles and contains the cognitive capacities of the mind and what allows them a relatively unencumbered expressive domain.

[24] This conception clearly has Protestant and Puritan roots. For a brief but illuminating discussion of these roots, see Hundert, "The Making of Homo-Faber," pp. 3–23. Also see Dunn, *Political Thought of John Locke*, pp. 245–61.

The topic most extensively considered in the *Thoughts* is that of the choice of a tutor for the child. I consider the issues mentioned above by reference to Locke's discussion of this topic. Unlike most other concerns on which Locke's discussion is scattered, on this topic he writes with continuous, systematic, and deliberate care. Nothing in "the whole business of education" deserves more careful attention, because its effects are so far-reaching and indelible, than the choice of a tutor. Locke is aware that good tutors can be expensive, but they are, he says, "a better purchase" than the addition of several acres of earth (p. 187). Locke in fact goes into some detail, elaborating on the various things it would be worth giving up to secure such a person.

With such weight attached to the introduction of the tutor, it is at the least surprising that, when Locke comes to specify the attributes of such a person, he picks the following: "Sobriety, temperance, tenderness, diligence and discretion" (p. 187). No mention is made of scholarly aptitude, learning, experience, or even competence as a teacher. Indeed, Locke explicitly disparages those who consider knowledge of Latin and logic or a university education significant attributes in a potential tutor: "Will that furniture [Latin, logic, university education] make him [the child] a fine gentleman? Or can it be expected, that he should be better bred, better skilled in the world" (p. 190).

At the broadest level, the task of the tutor, as of the parents, is to instill principles of virtue in the child's supple and compliant mind. Given this purpose, and given what Locke has already said about the importance of reputation, it is not surprising that the actual consideration of what and how tutors must go about their task is prefaced by the credentials they must bear. Indeed, much of Locke's discussion focuses on this particular consideration. Thus, we are told that the tutor must "himself be well-bred, understand the ways of carriage, the measures of civility [different forms of courtesy] in all the variety of persons, times and places." Later we are told that the tutor must be "skilled in the world" (p. 190).

When Locke finally takes up the issue of what this tutor is enjoined to do for the child, this is what he says: "The great work of a *governor* is to fashion the carriage, and form the mind; to settle in his pupil good habits, and the principles of virtue and wisdom" (p. 198). This involves exposing the child to the ways of the world. There are in the section of the *Thoughts* dealing with the tutor over a dozen references to "the world." In all of them, Locke's point is to emphasize the role of the tutor in elaborating the distinctions of rank, class, status, and geography and habituating an appropriate external and internal response to them. Consider the following:

> The only fence against the world is, a thorough knowledge of it; into which a young gentleman should be entered by degrees. . . . The scene should be gently opened, and his entrance made step by step, and the dangers pointed out that attend him, from the several degrees, tempers, designs and clubs of men. *He should be prepared to be shocked by some, and caressed by others; warn'd who are like to oppose, who to mislead, who to undermine him, and who to serve him.* He should be instructed how to know, and distinguish them. (P. 195)

The tutor's task in introducing and guiding a pupil through this world of enormous variety is not merely one of exposure. What Locke has in mind is not an innocent seventeenth-century analogue to leafing through a world atlas and being struck and perhaps a bit shocked by the distinct colors and shapes, even though the significance of the global perspective he emphasizes is not to be minimized.[25] What is sadly remarkable about such a passage is its pervasive sense of caution, its underlying parochialism, its strange and extreme defensiveness, the behavioral and emotional anticipation or preparedness it enjoins regarding the

[25] See George C. Brauer, *The Education of a Gentleman: Theories of Gentlemanly Education in England 1660–1775* (New York: New College and University Press, 1959), Chap. 4.

encounter with others and the world, and hence the subtle but unmistakable way it muffles and bleaches spontaneity—and all this directed at the mind of a child. One must wonder at the horrifying effects the three hundred odd travel books in Locke's personal library must have had on his own equanimity.

There are numerous other passages in which Locke all but explicitly reveals the prejudices of his class and wishes them inscribed on a child's early consciousness, as when he speaks explicitly of the requirements appropriate only to an English gentleman (pp. 197, 201). But such passages, because they express the crude sentiment of a class, are ultimately less revealing. Consider, however, this final example:

> He [the tutor] should acquaint him [the child] with the true state of the world. Thus by safe and insensible degrees, he will pass from boy to a man; which is the most hazardous step in all the whole course of life. This therefore should be carefully watched, and a young man with great diligence handed over it; and not, as now usually is done, be taken from a governor's conduct, and all at once thrown into the world upon his own, not without manifest danger of immediate spoiling; there being nothing more frequent, than instances of the great looseness, extravagancy and debauchery, which young men have run into as soon as they have been let lose from a severe and strict education: which, I think, may be chiefly imputed to their wrong way of breeding. (P. 193)

Here again one has that same emotional posture of cowering at the world lest the tutor be unexpectedly removed and the child find himself helplessly driven to extravagance, debauchery, and looseness. On a boy's transition to adulthood, Locke, it appears, can only express worry about the hazards involved. To know the true state of the world and to be rational about it is to know caution and safety and to acknowledge the manifest danger. To be free in such a world is to act in light of this rational knowledge. It is not surprising that Locke finds not simply in Latin, Greek, and logic but also in mathematics and the knowledge of languages a pale defense against such perilous odds. Nor is it surprising that he should prefer instead a tutor who "knows the world well; the ways, the humors, the follies, the cheats, the faults of the age" (p. 192).

For Locke, to be confronted by this world is not to be open to its diversity, to its often incommensurable and even inaccessible norms and the different ways of finding one's place in it. Instead, the purpose of being exposed to it, within the embrace of a familiar authority relationship (and one must wonder if Locke would have encouraged such exposure in the first place had it not by his time become an unavoidable reality with visible benefits for other reasons), is to be able to fashion a response to it in advance of the actual encounter. This response in advance is not one in which the child and the adult are expected to face the hazards of the world with a sense of potential mastery, a confidence that by an act of will, judgment, or discrimination they will be able to impose order on this world. Strangely, Locke's children will neither accept the world for what it is or may be nor respond to it with an indifference born of self-confidence. Instead, they will find their places in it by leaning against the solidity of private dispositions that are no more than the hardened surface of habits instilled in them before they could think, remember, and hence reconsider. When they discipline themselves, they will do so in view of some authority to whom they must submit, acting again on the habitual association the authority embodies, linking self-discipline and submission. When they express deep private judgments of people, situations, and places, they will manifest the burden of an ingrained pusillanimity that knows judgment only by reference to the esteem and disgrace they may bring them in the eyes of others. In brief, when they express their individuality in private or in consenting to political authority, or even in demanding that a particular government be overthrown in view of the violation of the trust on which it was authorized, they will be expressing, if Locke's education has the permanent effects it is designed to have, the various abridgments and compromises through which they came to be and see themselves as individual.

The Political Compromise of Individuality

I now briefly return to the *Second Treatise*, not to analyze Locke's institutional proposals in all their richness and complexity, but to recapitulate the claims made with respect to the *Thoughts* by reference to snatches from the *Second Treatise*. It may rightly be complained that, even if one accepts the foregoing analysis, one cannot simply assume that Locke's prescriptions for the education of young children constitute the normative ideal of his political proposals. The fact that Locke encourages individuality in children only on the condition that its expression assume a truncated form cannot, it might be said, conclude our view of this ideal for citizens. I mean to respond to this objection by pointing to the ways the conception of individuality articulated in the previous section is, in fact, recapitulated in the *Second Treatise*. That said, I do not deny that my reading of the *Second Treatise* is itself informed by my reading of the *Thoughts*.

At the outset of the *Second Treatise*, Locke, while discussing the state of nature, suggests that there is a fundamental link, to which I have made earlier reference, between the law of nature and individual human reason (pp. 288–89). He goes on in the same chapter to state that it is not only "certain that there is such a law [of nature]" but also "intelligible and plain to a rational Creature, and a Studier of that Law" (p. 293). He continues by stating that the law of nature is indeed the basis for most municipal laws. All these claims underscore the link between human reason, positive laws, and the law of nature. It is, therefore, noteworthy that the fourth chapter, "Of Slavery," is introduced with the following formulation:

> The *Natural Liberty* of Man is to be free from any Superior Power on Earth, and not to be under the Will or Legislative Authority of Man, but to have only the Law of Nature for his Rule. The *Liberty of Man, in Society,* is to be under no other Legislative Power, but that established, by consent, in the common-wealth, nor under the dominion of any Will, or Restraint of any Law, but what the Legislative shall enact, according to the trust put in it. (P. 301)

Locke's formulation of natural liberty is characteristically expansive. Human being are by nature free from the authority of every terrestrial power including, as Locke explicitly states, the power of a legislative authority. It is revealing that even the law of nature is not presented as an authority that curbs human freedom but rather as a rule that directs it. In contrast, while speaking of liberty in society, Locke immediately resorts to the more severe metaphor of being *under* an authority. In society, we are told, freedom is restrained by the consented authority of the legislature. Moreover, there is no reference to the law of nature as either a rule or an authoritative constraint. This formulation is striking in that it intimates something Locke later states explicitly, namely, the degree to which in moving from the natural state into the commonwealth, humans surrender their natures. In contrast to natural liberty, which stands defiant of any authority, we have what Locke calls the "Freedom of Men under Government" to "have a standing Rule to live by, common to everyone of that Society, and made by the Legislative Power." In the course of one brief paragraph the natural liberty of man to be free from "any Superior Power on Earth" has been reduced to a "Liberty to follow [one's] own Will" only where the "Rule prescribes not" (p. 302).

A similar though more explicit equivocation of freedom and

the law of nature is to be found in Locke's discussion of parental power. Unlike Adam, who was created in a state of physical and mental perfection and whose actions were therefore thoroughly in conformity with the dictates of the law of nature, human beings have, as Locke puts it, "another way of entrance into the World." But, despite this difference, they are governed by the same law that governed Adam. Because of their natural birth, however, a birth

> that produced them ignorant and without the use of *Reason*, they were not presently *under that Law*: for no Body can be under a Law, which is not promulgated to him; and this Law being promulgated or made known by *Reason* only, he that is not come to the Use of his *Reason*, cannot be said to be *under his Law*; and *Adam's* Children being not presently as soon as born, *under this Law of Reason* were not presently *free*. For *Law*, in its true Notion, is not so much the Limitation as *the direction of a free and intelligent Agent* to his proper Interest, and prescribes no farther than is for the general Good of those under that law. (P. 323)

It is clear that we are born ignorant and devoid of reason. It is this deficiency in our reason that temporarily makes us unable to be "under" the law of nature. But here Locke equivocates. He states first that nobody can be under a law "which is not promulgated to him" and then immediately further qualifies it by the words "and this Law being promulgated or made known by Reason only." The addition of the words "or made known by Reason" seriously modifies his meaning, for if the law of nature were simply promulgated to us, we could think of it as some authoritative version of Christian precepts. Natural law would, on this understanding, simply constitute the objective ground for our actions. The status of moral good and evil would as such be antecedent to any act of human interpretation.[26] But by

[26] This was the view held among the Cambridge Platonists, such as Fowler, Rust, and most important, Cudworth.

introducing another means of access to the precepts of natural law, one might think that Locke is opening the door for a host of subjective interpretations and thus effectively subverting the law's objective status. Indeed, to the extent that what individuals take to be reason or reasonable varies, it is unclear that such an interpretation can be resisted. This is precisely the spirit in which Strauss identifies Locke as undermining natural law by surreptitiously evacuating it of any objective authority. But Strauss's interpretation ignores the possibility that Locke is presuming that reason, and hence the interpretation of natural law based on reason, is uniform. If, however, one interprets such a passage in light of the *Thoughts* and recognizes the extent to which the pedagogical project articulated there attempts to mold or homogenize individual reason, then the effect of making natural law contingent on human reason is hardly subversive to those laws. If Locke has opened the door to a subjective reading of natural law, he has also tried to ensure that those who go through that door will fix on natural law much the same interpretation.

This reading based on the *Thoughts* carries over and casts a distinct light on Locke's claim that one's man's freedom "is *grounded* on his having *reason*, which is able to instruct him in that law he is to govern himself by, and make him know how far he is left to the freedom of his own will" (*Thoughts*, p. 352) or his claim "*where there is no Law, there is no Freedom*" (*Second Treatise*, p. 324). Having announced this general claim, Locke immediately restricts the connotations of what he now calls liberty to a considerably narrower domain. He states, "For *Liberty* is to be free from restraint and violence from other which cannot be, where there is no Law" (p. 324). Striking is the sudden reference to the restraint and violence of others to secure against which, we are told, law is necessary. But only a couple of chapters earlier, Locke declares that natural liberty "was to follow [one's] own Will in all things" (p. 302). In fact, Locke in the very next line reinvokes this more expansive notion of freedom, but now it is negatively qualified:

> But freedom is not as we are told, *A Liberty for every man to do as he lists:* (For who could be free when every other Man's Humor might domineer over him?) But a *Liberty* to dispose, and order, as he lists, his Person, Actions, Possessions, and his whole Property, within the Allowance of those Laws under which he is; and therein not to be subject to the arbitrary Will of another, but freely follow his own. (P. 324)

There is a curious nervousness in Locke's language. What is stated parenthetically and discarded with rhetorical flourish as though it were a marginal concern is in fact central. Precisely because at a natural level the potential of the individual threatens to defy any restriction on its freedom, it cannot be conveniently marginalized. Its potential must be husbanded; it must be curbed by a law. But this law must itself be cognizant of the defiance of law that characterized the nature of the natural individual. In this conundrum, we can see the paradoxical role of law and freedom that structures Locke's enterprise. By the nature of the individual involved, Locke cannot expect or demand moderation. He cannot, in the manner of Plato, announce *sophrosyne* (temperance) as an essential virtue. Nor can the arbitrary will of this subject be allowed to fully express itself with all its immoderate potential. The law that is to curb the arbitrary expressions of this will cannot therefore be too distant or elevated from the subject's interests. Admittedly, we are still not in the presence of Kant's self-legislating moral subject, who is noumenally free only to find that in that realm one must tyrannize oneself with the iron fist of a self-prescribed universal law. But in the strained language of Locke's prose, we see how the freedom of the will must be curbed without being openly dominated. When Locke at the end of the passage just cited says that liberty is the ability to freely follow one's will, the will he has in mind is one that has (so Locke hopes) been carefully clipped of its subjective and imaginative potential by law and by a program of education. What started out at the beginning of the paragraph as the *law* which without limiting gave *direction* to free and intelligent agents is now a group of *laws within* whose *allowance* agents may follow their wills. The apparently minor shift from the singular "law" to the plural "laws" is in fact a momentous change, strongly reminiscent of the change effected in the child by the inculcation of not only self-restraint but an outlook of submission alloyed with such restraint.

It is worth recalling that the passages being discussed all come from the chapter on paternal power, in which, as in the *Thoughts*, the theme of freedom, submission, or governance (as Locke calls it in the chapter) and a deep conventionalism are run together. As an aside, it should be noted that the title of this chapter is a puzzle, and an abiding conventionalism may cast some light on this puzzle. Locke starts the chapter with a pointed diatribe against the characterization of education as a paternal responsibility. Both "reason and revelation" make clear that it is in fact a responsibility and power "equal to both the concurrent causes of it" (p. 321)—Locke's way of referring to fathers and mothers. And yet, despite this clearheaded disquisition, Locke strangely titles his own chapter "Of Paternal Power." At any rate, parental power and obligation has its purpose in "inform[ing] the Mind and govern[ing] the Actions of their yet ignorant Nonage, till Reason shall take its place, and ease them of that Trouble" (p. 324). To this general purpose Locke immediately gives a more specific and political content. The task of the parents is to nurture their children to the state of freedom wherein they may will for themselves. Until that stage is reached, the parents must *understand* and will for their children (p. 324). But consider Locke's language as he speaks of the moment a child comes to reason for himself and sheds the "swaddling cloths" of parental support—the moment when he becomes free. Locke celebrates this moment as a

> State of Maturity wherein he [the child] might be suppos'd capable to know that Law, that so he might keep his Actions

within the Bounds of it. When he has acquired that State, he is
presumed to know how far that Law is to be his Guide, and
how far he may make use of his Freedom, . . . to know how far
the Law allows a liberty. (P. 325)

This is Locke's understanding of the obligation parents have to
their children. It is to ensure that by the age of twenty-one their
progeny are suitably inculcated with a reason that proscribes and
prescribes to the inclinations of the will. It is not surprising that
the verb Locke uses most to speak of the will is that of *grounding*.
His injunctions to parents refer almost exclusively to this single
issue of curbing the willful desires and passions of their children
so that the child may "never [be] let loose to the disposure of his
own Will (because he knows no bound to it)" (pp. 325–26). If
these injunctions, along with their more detailed explication in
the *Thoughts*, are taken as the basis from which to interpret
statements such as "where there is no law, there is no freedom,"
one can see how they may not be precursors to a conception of
autonomy evident in Kant's rationalism but rather successors to
a pedagogical and domesticated Hobbesian conception of awe
and fear.

For the remainder of this chapter, I limit myself to a discussion
of some of the explicitly political moves that characterize Locke's
thought in the *Second Treatise*. The central question with which I
am concerned is, to what extent can Locke politically accommodate the individual whose provenance he has articulated?

Enough has been said in the previous chapter about the transgressive frenzy of the Lockean individual in a natural state. Here
I focus on the problem presented by the compacted abundance
of the subject's natural yet distinctly political description. After
writing "*where there is no law, there is no freedom*," Locke states,

But Because no *Political Society* can be, nor subsist without
having in it self the Power to preserve the Property, and in
order thereunto punish the Offences of all those of that Society; there, and there only is *Political Society*, where everyone

of the Members hath quitted this natural Power, resign'd it up into the hands of the Community in all cases. . . . And thus all private judgement of every particular Member being excluded, the Community comes to be Umpire, by settled standing Rules. (P. 342)

It is obvious from this passage that we have moved to another realm. What is less obvious and less noted is that we have also moved to another subject. More precisely, the move to a new realm is made possible by the recasting of the subject. Both changes are signaled by the grammatical contrast instituted by the first word, "but." The natural Lockean subjects with whom we are familiar have been denatured. This radical metamorphosis is expressed by an equally radical terminology. They have *quit* their natural power, *resigned* it without exception to the community and in the process excluded their own *judgment*. Only on the basis of this severe sequestering of their nature can they make the move into the commonwealth. From this passage one could conclude that the commonwealth as an artifice was forged through an act of collective self-sacrifice. Moreover, it appears to be a sacrifice in which what is gained was already present to start with, namely, the right to property and the capacity to punish against its offense.

There is another significant change, linguistically at least it bears a resemblance to the classical question of the one and the many. The many *members* in their act of quitting have formed *one* political society, the private judgments of *every* particular member being excluded, *the community* comes to be umpire, and further on in the same passage those who are united form *one body*. The frenzy and the dense political capacities that characterized subjects in their natural state all appear to have been reduced in scale and energy. The political seems distinctly more focused. By the consented act of denaturing themselves, subjects appear almost effortlessly to have obviated the threat of the state of war.

Let us pause and return to our subject as we knew him and see if we can recognize him through the garb he now wears. Put differently, is there anything in his present state that bears the signature of his former nature? Toward this end let us consider two passages:

> The Judgments of the Commonwealth . . . which indeed are his own Judgments, they being made by himself, or his representative.

> For hereby he authorizes the Society, or which is all one, the Legislative thereof to make laws for him as the publick good of the Society shall require. (P. 343)

In these two passages Locke is dealing with two different sets of activities. In the first passage it is the judgments of the individual and the judgments of the commonwealth. In the second it is the authority of the individual and the authority of society. It is clear that Locke recognizes the distinct possibilities within each of the two sets; that is, he has admitted to the judgments of an individual being different from those of a commonwealth, and likewise to the authority of the individual being distinct from that of society. But, despite this recognition of their differences, Locke claims that they are in fact now identical. The judgments of the commonwealth, we are told, are "his own" (the individual's); "the Legislative" and the authority of the individual "is all one." Yet we know from the preceding passage that a radical change has in fact been affected. Man had quit his private judgments and given up his particular authority. And so we must ask, how despite this change—despite the severity of the subject's denaturing—he identifies his former self in the judgments of the commonwealth and in the authority of the legislative.

To this question there is an apparently obvious answer—that since the commonwealth and legislative are political artifices forged through consent, they therefore represent those whose consent they embody.[27] But this proffered answer only begs the question. Since in the compact to join and create political society natural subjects resigned and quit their nature, we face the question, who is it that is being represented? More fully, the question I am concerned with is, how is it that subjects who were so conspicuously marked by subjective anthropological potential are now sufficiently trimmed to be representable.[28]

Thus formulated, it is clear that the question I am pursuing is both political and psychological. It is political because Locke, as Hobbes before him, has clearly established that it relates to issues of public safety and public order. It is psychological because the issue of representation involves subjects who, to secure their safety, may have to surrender their nature. In a sense this entire work is an attempt to wrestle with this paradox—a paradox I take to have configured Locke's entire project and much of subsequent liberal thought. This is not, however, to suggest that Locke is aware of this paradox. Indeed, I shortly suggest how its sustained denial crucially jeopardizes his political prescriptions. But, though he does not, in my view, recognize it, he does supply the pieces that go into its articulation.[29]

We have seen that Locke presents us with a situation in which both a difference and an identity are suggested. The former

[27] See Martin Seliger, *The Liberal Politics of John Locke* (London: Allen and Unwin, 1968), pp. 294–300, and W. Cassinelli, "The Consent of the Governed," *Western Political Quarterly* 12, no. 2 (1959), 406–7.

[28] Hanna Pitkin's brilliant book *The Concept of Representation* (Berkeley: University of California Press, 1972) addresses a question different from the one being pursued here. In brief, this difference lies in her concern with "an idea, a concept, a word," in contrast to my concern with the political psychology of the individual who must be represented and the degree to which the institutions of representation comport with this political psychology.

[29] Despite obvious and important differences, there is, I think, an analogy between Locke's understanding of representation and Kant's bifurcated moral subject; see Bernard Williams, *Moral Luck* (Cambridge: Cambridge University Press, 1981), especially the chapters "Internal and External Reasons" and "The Ought of Moral Obligation." Also see Sandel, *Limits of Liberal Justice*, chaps. 1 and 2.

refers to the radical change required of subjects to warrant their entry into the commonwealth and the latter to Locke's claim that, despite this change, subjects remain at least in respect of their judgments unchanged. To say that this tension is settled by the notion of representation is at best only partially true, for subjects can be only partially represented. This Locke has himself indirectly admitted by recognizing that, in the move from the state of nature to the commonwealth, the former has lost its subjective variety and plurality (members joining to form one body). Clearly, the focused unity the commonwealth purports to create is possible only if the extremism and multiplicity of judgments that characterized the state of nature are, as it were, leveled out. In Locke's views on education we have seen this need expressed in its most candid form. Reason, we have heard him say, must be disciplined to curb "the tempers" of an "unrestrain'd nature." Representation, I am suggesting, performs the same task. But, whereas education attempts to recast subjective nature by its persistence, representation conceals it by its limited liberality. Harvey Mansfield in an essay on Hobbes succinctly expresses this: "Representative government thus seems to be a metaphor in which we say that the laws imposed on us came from ourselves, because the artificial man acts for the natural man."[30] But for Hobbes, who is unabashedly dualist regarding natural and artificial human being, this is not an embarrassing revelation. It is merely the conclusion of a theorem that set out to establish and ensure self-preservation. In contrast, it commits Locke to a dualism which, because it is unacknowledged, leads to the mischaracterization of the subject. By this I mean that we cannot recognize in the citizens who inhabit the latter part of the *Second Treatise* any semblance of the transgressive vitality that characterized them in their natural state. Instead we find them leveled out, carefully

---

[30] Harvey C. Mansfield, Jr., "Hobbes and the Science of Indirect Government," *American Political Science Review*, 65 (1971), 109.

regulated, and utterly devoid of "overweening passions" and "arbitrary desires." Let us consider some inconspicuous examples, which are especially revealing because they lack the quality that made Hume most suspicious of Locke—"philosophical refinement."[31]

At the beginning of the chapter entitled "Of Political or Civil Society," Locke discusses what he refers to as "conjugal society." The purpose of this discussion has rightly been identified as being to break the Filmerian analogy between absolute rule in the family and in the polity.[32] But Locke's language in this discussion is revealing beyond its ostensible purpose. *"Conjugal Society,"* we are told,

> is made by a voluntary Compact between Man and Woman: And tho' it consists chiefly in such a Communion and Right in one another Bodies, as is necessary to its Chief End, Procreation; yet it draws with it mutual Support, and Assistance, and a Communion of Interest too, as necessary not only to unite their Care, and Affection, but also necessary to their common Off-spring, . . .
>
> For the end of *conjunction between Male and Female,* being not barely Procreation, but the continuance of the Species, this conjunction betwixt Male and Female ought to last, even after Procreation . . .
>
> And herein I think lies the chief, if not the only reason, *why the Male and Female in Mankind are tied to a longer conjunction, viz.* because the Female is capable of conceiving. (Pp. 337–38)

This is Locke's characterization of marriage. It is, we are told. a compact, which communicates rights to one another's bodies. It

---

[31] David Hume, "Of the Original Contract," in *Social Contract: Essays by Locke, Hume and Rousseau,* ed. Ernest Barker (New York: Oxford University Press, 1948), p. 153.

[32] See, for instance, Geraint Parry, "Individuality, Politics and the Critique of Paternalism in John Locke," *Political Studies* 12, no. 2 (1964), 172, and Selinger, *Liberal Politics of John Locke,* p. 211.

has a chief end, namely, the continuation of the species. Locke even suggests that this may be its only purpose. It is not between a man and a woman but between a male and a female. Reluctantly Locke admits the obvious, that it involves care and affection, but even this is directed to a purpose, the common offspring. Locke's language is painfully instrumental. It is utterly devoid of anything vaguely akin to the free play of the romantic urge. Surely, even by the Puritan standards of his time, this characterization of marriage is cold and lifeless to the point of being offensive. There is not a hint of spontaneity. Marriage, we are led to believe, has a clinical regularity. Yet it is paradigmatically an act of voluntary compact. Can we in this understanding of voluntary recognize the "expanded subject?" More important, would this subject settle for the implications of this usage?

Let us consider another briefer example from the same chapter. Locke states, "For where-ever any two Men are, who have no standing Rule, and common Judge to Appeal to on Earth for the determination of Controversies of Right betwixt them, there they are still *in the state of Nature*, and under all the inconveniences of it" (p. 344). Two aspects of this passage are striking. One is the hurried manner in which Locke arrives at his conclusion and another, the implications of the conclusion itself. In the chapter on the state of nature, Locke had stated that "Truth and keeping of Faith belong to Men, as Men, and not as Members of Society" (p. 295). Yet in the commonwealth the mere lack of a standing rule and a common judge immediately precipitate the inconveniences of the state of nature. But what if the two men were friends, perhaps comrades, perhaps fellow-believers or brothers? All these possibilities have been hurriedly overlooked, not through mere oversight but rather due to a precise political posture. It is a posture that requires an uncompromising denaturing of the subject so much so that even truth and keeping faith must now be replaced by standing rules and common judges.

In studying these two examples, I have tried to draw out some of the implications of the denaturing of the subject which are required for his or her entry into political societies. The examples, I think, establish that the denaturing is indeed uncompromising. Citizens of the commonwealth would not only be unable to recognize their former expansive selves but would in fact have no memory of them: Locke tells us that "Government is every where antecedent to records" and that any knowledge of the original is merely accidental (p. 352).

From the perspective we have reached it is possible to see how the political society made necessary by the subjective potential of the Lockean subject in turn excludes precisely this potential. The expanded boundaries of the subject can be accommodated neither by natural law nor by representation and its cognate institutions, except by a theoretical feint. The radical sequestering of the subject's nature is indeed a precondition for his or her political identity. Perhaps this is not surprising, for the need for political society arose from the intersubjective problem of the negotiation of personal boundaries. The quest for a common judge is also the search for a yardstick that allows these boundaries to be established without problematizing what is enclosed within them; that is, the expanded subject is conjured as the problem for the establishment of political society, but without an assuaging of the subject's nature itself. When Locke announces that the judgments of the commonwealth are "his own," he betrays the subject on whose behalf he had challenged Filmerian absolutism. Or maybe one should say that the subject has proved to be too overbearing a client to find in Locke a worthy patron.

CHAPTER FIVE

Conclusion

In this work I have attempted to elaborate a distinct problematic from which to fashion an understanding of Locke and, by association, of liberalism more generally. The familiar naturalistic perspective is one that identifies both Locke and liberalism with an overriding concern to settle problems of public order and individual rights, and one that views these problems as stemming from a natural tendency among individuals to follow their appetites and thus invade each other's turf and create public disorder. Within this perspective, the meaning of human individuality is taken for granted or, at least, settled by notions such as that human beings are naturally free, rational, and equal. What is in need of theoretical articulation, what Locke is assumed to be concerned with, and what subsequent liberals have manifestly been concerned with is a framework that justifies a political authority that comports with the rights of individuals.

In contrast to this focus on the conflicts among individuals as a result of their appetitive nature, I have emphasized the cognitive dimension or what might, in contrast with the problems of intersubjectivity, be thought of as the problems of intrasubjectivity. The two perspectives are not in a fundamental way mutually exclusive, even though in their details they may not at all points be reconcilable. In any case, such broad commensurability of detail depends on the particulars of two or more given interpretations. At any rate, within the perspective I am offering or emphasizing, a distinct set of problems are animated. Instead of presuming the coherence of individuality by reference to human freedom, rationality, and equality, I see Locke as involved in trying to specify the content of these terms in view of the restive nature of our natural cognitive expressions. Put differently, instead of seeing Locke and liberalism as articulating the framework and institutions through which a pent-up natural individuality finds expression, I have suggested that Locke is involved in constructing a particular form and venue for individuality. Venues in this sense guide but equally important they also constrain.

Thus, my purpose has been to reveal the mechanisms by which the vagrance, the excesses, and the frenzy that buffet this self are molded. I have spoken of this as the process of forming individuality. The sense in which this term captures Locke's endeavor needs to be specified; the term carries a multiplicity of connotations, and it is clear that Locke's attempts to firm up individuality in one sense undermine it in another. In the face of the natural self's absence of self-control, Locke wants a self-disciplined and directed individual. Given the porous and tenuous boundaries between the madman and his sober counterpart, Locke wants to place unmistakable distinctions. Given the fluidity of contrast between the use and abuse of words, between them being the vehicle through which we express our "ideas" and the ravings of our imagination, he wants to again place unmistakable markers.

The forging of individuality is tied to the consolidation of these distinctions. But for these distinctions to be consolidated, either they must be extant or they must be created. It would be a nonsensical exaggeration to suggest that Locke is responding to a situation of complete social and psychological evacuation in which all organizing categories and distinctions are hopelessly ambiguous. Even during times of enormous upheaval, when the quotidian assurances of life are lifted from their mundane grooves and held up to the gaze of transforming scrutiny, there remain values, traditions, and practices—even if only contested ones. What Locke is involved in is reworking these preexisting norms into alternative frames with distinct dichotomies informed by novel imperatives. To put it differently, individuality is what is valorized in the process of constructing and sequestering normality from what one might loosely call social and individual pathology.

These are not Locke's terms, but what they suggest is evident in the tenacity with which Locke tries to firm up the distinction between the mad and the insane, despite the absence of any natural demarcations between them. The construction of individuality is intertwined with the construction of a broader ideal of normality. By recognizing this kinship, one can see how the problem represented by individuality is reinscribed as a problem of conduct, of making vivid the boundaries between acceptable and unacceptable behavior, between reason and madness, where all these distinctions have to be illuminated without invoking the essentialism of Aristotelian or Thomistic naturalism.

Locke's response to the subjectivity of the self is an elaborate regime of individual and social discipline, a specification and encouragment of conformity with norms through early habituation and a promotion of predictability through enforced and encouraged regularity. For Locke, individuals are formed by embedding them within, and by their internalizing, the minutiae of a complex constellation of social structures and conventional norms. This is an individuality that requires the enforcement of and allegiance to a host of semicodified cultural and conventional distinctions. It is, in brief, predicated on what Durkheim called "logical conformity," the process by which societies reproduce themselves by rigorously organizing the perception of the social order.[1] Hence it is an individuality that views the unmolded will

---

[1] E. Durkheim, *The Elementary Forms of Religious Life* (London: Allen and Unwin, 1915), p. 17. Also see Durkheim's almost completely ignored yet remarkable work *The Evolution of Educational Thought*, trans. Peter Collins (Boston: Routledge & Kegan Paul, 1977), especially pp. 252–348.

with utmost suspicion—that will which Nietzsche celebrated and identified with "something complicated" because it required "getting away from the feeling of a condition to a muscularity of feelings," and which was thus the basis of eccentricity, power, and an inner certainty that demanded obedience.[2] This is the will that would always resist, as oxymoronic, its mutation into notions such as "the general will," the "collective will," or the "national will."

In contrast, I have claimed that for Locke individuality turns on an avid affirmation of the commonality, the transparency, and, when pressed to its extreme, even the uniformity of people. These commitments might appear to resonate with the solidaristic and organic spirit of ancient and medieval thought and practice; the appearance is deeply misleading. The organic emphasis in Plato, Aquinas, and even Burke values the fit and social coherence of hierarchically ordered groupings of individuals with distinct identities. It is thus predicated on a recognition of fundamental and, in Plato's case, psychologically essentialist differences among people. In Locke, the solidaristic commitments stem from a negative valuation of the subjective potential of individuals. Hence, ironically, individuality is Locke's response to the threat posed by this subjectivity. Louis Hartz, in interpreting America through Locke makes the following observation and in the process reveals something essential about Locke himself: "Amid the 'free air' of American life, something new appeared: men began to be held together not by the knowledge that they were different parts of a corporate whole, but by the knowledge that they were similar participants in a uniform way of life."[3] When self-discipline becomes alloyed with submission, privacy with reputation, an involvement with the world with a preformulated and ingrained response to it, the outcome may, indeed, be a uniform way of life. And the uniformity, in such instances, is not

[2] Friedrich Nietzsche, *Beyond Good and Evil* (New York: Vintage Books, 1966), no. 19.

[3] Louis Hartz, *Liberal Tradition in America*, p. 55.

simply at the level of expressive or manifest behavior; rather, is it the expression of a deeper, private uniformity.

One face of Lockean liberalism is deeply suspicious of that which smacks of being fundamentally different, especially if that difference claims for itself immunity on grounds of privacy. Such alterity rekindles the anxieties Locke felt toward the unmolded, natural self.[4] America, where the legal right to privacy—where, to invoke the words of Justices Brandeis and Blackmun, the right to be left alone, to make intimate choices within the space of one's home is, at best, uncertain, and where the tenuousness of these rights is not taken "by the majority" to implicate what it means to be an individual—may, once again, reveal a truth implicit in Locke.[5] The basis of Lockean individuality can indeed undermine it to the point that even individuality becomes, as Georges Santayana felt it was in America, something compulsory.[6]

There is a thin and no doubt shifting line which, to put it in Tocquevillean terms, distinguishes a situation in which the shared mores of a society nourish and enrich the spirit of liberty and one in which they prescribe and regiment the terms by which that spirit must be expressed. My purpose is not to claim that Locke's liberalism ineluctably tends toward the latter, darker side of that line. Such a determination would in any case depend on the nuances of a particular context, and mere textual

---

[4] I briefly consider this theme with respect to Locke and more extensively with respect to nineteenth-century British liberals in Uday S. Mehta, "Liberal Strategies of Exclusion," *Politics and Society* 18, no. 4 (1990), 427–54. Also see the extremely thoughtful article by Kirstie M. McClure, "Difference, Diversity, and the Limits of Toleration," *Political Theory* 18, no. 3 (1990), 361–91.

[5] See *Olmstead v. United States*, 277 U.S. 438 (1928), Brandeis, J., dissenting; *Bowers v. Hardwick* 478 U.S. 186 (1986) and *Webster v. Reproductive Health Services* 109 S. Ct. 3040 (1989), Blackmun J., dissenting.

[6] George Santayana, *Character and Opinion in the United States* (New York: Scribner, 1924), p. 210: "Even what is best in America is compulsory, the idealism, the zeal, the beautiful unison of its great moments."

interpretation should demur from presuming on such contextual particulars. But it has been my purpose to reveal the sense in which the framing of Locke's problematic and his response to it allow for a compromise of the very individuality with which he is so often associated.

This aspect of Locke's liberalism is eclipsed if one considers him exclusively as a theorist concerned with delineating the rights of individuals and defining the corresponding limits on political authority. Such an emphasis obscures the governance involved in constructing the individual whose rights this perspective considers. The distorting effects of this focus is not simply one of emphasis. By overlooking the process of formation, one overlooks the manner and extent to which individuality and its potential have been qualified, homogenized, and constricted in the course of this process itself. By this oversight, one is committed to look to political society and its institutions as the exclusive forum in which individuality is advanced, confined, or otherwise effected—and hence one returns to the overvaluation of Locke as a theorist who not only limits the ambit of political power but himself is concerned with the limited issue of political power.

It is to Locke's credit that he acknowledges the kinship between madness and sobriety, reason and imagination, and that he acknowledges them as aspects to which we are all prone. Such a predicament could have furnished the foundation of an individuality that celebrated and cultivated singularity, dissonance, and ultimate disagreements. But Locke's response to his own acknowledgment is like the response he encourages in the child faced by a strange world, a response in which he cowers at the implications of such singularity. Individuality in Locke can become, as indeed it has become in so many liberal societies, the expression of a stance toward oneself and the world in which the willful, the eccentric, and the mysterious have all been carefully sanitized and calibrated—and through such a process rendered free, rational, and equal. In a world that is, once again, exploding with ethnic, gender, national, and subnational commitments, such an outlook may be an expression not only of weakness but, equally important, of an outmoded complacency in which one naively presumes that all differences will become familiar.

Bibliography

Aaron, Richard. *John Locke.* Oxford: Clarendon Press, 1955.

Aarsleff, Hans. "Locke's Reputation in Nineteenth Century England." *The Monist* 55 (1971), 409.

Ashcraft, Richard. *Revolutionary Politics and Locke's Two Treatises of Government.* Princeton: Princeton University Press, 1986.

Auerbach, Erich. *Mimesis: The Representation of Reality in Western Literature.* Trans. W. R. Trask. Princeton: Princeton University Press, 1974.

Bercovich, Sacvan. *The Puritan Origins of the American Self.* New Haven: Yale University Press, 1975.

Berlin, Isaiah. "Rationality of Value Judgments." In *Nomos,* vol. 7: *Rational Decision,* ed. C. J. Friedrich. New York: New York University Press, 1964.

——. *Four Essays on Liberty.* Oxford: Oxford University Press, 1979.

Blumenberg, Hans. *The Legitimacy of the Modern Age.* Trans. R. M. Wallace. Cambridge: MIT Press, 1983.

Bourdieu, Pierre. *Distinction: A Social Critique of the Judgment of Taste.* London: Routledge & Kegan Paul, 1984.

——. *The Logic of Practice.* Trans. Richard Nice. Stanford: Stanford University Press, 1990.

Bourne, F. H. R. *The Life of John Locke.* London: 1867.

Brauer, George C. *The Education of a Gentleman: Theories of Gentleman Education in England, 1660–1775.* New York: New College and University Press, 1959.

Brown, Peter. *Society and the Holy in Late Antiquity.* Berkeley: University of California Press, 1982.

Butler, Judith. "The Force of Fantasy: Feminism, Mapplethorpe, and Discursive Excess." *Differences* 2 (Summer 1990), 105–25.

———. *Gender Trouble: Feminism and the Subversion of Identity.* New York: Routledge, 1990.

Carlton, Frank. *Economic Influences upon Educational Progress in the United States, 1820–1850.* New York: Teacher's College Press, 1966.

Cassinelli, W. "The Consent of the Governed." *Western Political Quarterly* 12, no. 2 (1959), 406–7.

Cohen, Joshua. "Democratic Equality." *Ethics* 99 (July 1989), 727–51.

———. "Autonomy, Security and Authority: Hobbes's Defense of Absolutism." Unpublished manuscript. Political Science Department, M.I.T.

Connolly, William. *Political Theory and Modernity.* New York: Basil Blackwell, 1988.

Cranston, Maurice. *John Locke: A Biography.* London: Longmans, Green, 1957.

Cumming, Robert D. *Human Nature and History.* Chicago: University of Chicago Press, 1969.

DePorte, Michael V. *Nightmares and Hobbyhorses: Swift, Sterne and Augustan Ideas of Madness.* San Marino, Calif.: Huntington Library, 1974.

Descartes, René. *The Method, Meditations and Philosophy of Descartes.* Ed. and trans. John Veitch. New York: Tudor, 1937.

Dewhurst, Kenneth. *John Locke (1632–1704) Physician and Philosopher: A Medical Biography.* London: Wellcome Historical Medical Library, 1963.

Dunn, John. *The Political Thought of John Locke: An Historical Account of the Argument of the "Two Treatises of Government".* New York: Cambridge University Press, 1969.

Durkheim, E. *The Elementary Forms of Religious Life.* London: Allen and Unwin, 1915.

———. *The Evolution of Educational Thought.* Trans. Peter Collins. Boston: Routledge & Kegan Paul, 1977.

Dworkin, Andrea. *Pornography: Men Possessing Women.* New York: Seal, 1981.

Elias, Norbert. *The Civilizing Process: Power and Civility.* Trans. Edmund Jephcott. New York: Pantheon Books, 1982.

———. *The Court Society.* Trans. Edmund Jephcott. New York: Pantheon Books, 1983.

Filmer, Sir Robert. *Patriarcha and Other Political Works.* Ed. Peter Laslett. Oxford: Basil Blackwell, 1949.

Finnis, John. *Natural Law and Natural Rights.* Oxford: Clarendon Press, 1980.

Flathman, Richard. *The Philosophy and Politics of Freedom.* Chicago: University of Chicago Press, 1987.

Foucault, Michel. *Discipline and Punish*. Trans. Alan Sheridan. New York: Vintage Books, 1979.

——. "Sexuality and Solitude." In *On Signs*, ed. Marshall Blonsky. Baltimore: Johns Hopkins University Press, 1985.

——. *Madness and Civilization*. Trans. Richard Howard. New York: Vintage Books, 1988.

——. "Technologies of the Self." In *Technologies of the Self*, ed. Luther H. Martin, Huck Gutman, and Patrick H. Hutton. Amherst: University of Massachusetts Press, 1988.

Freud, Sigmund. *An Autobiographical Sketch*. Trans. James Strachey. New York: Norton, 1952.

——. *Group Psychology and the Analysis of the Ego*. Trans. James Strachey. New York: Norton, 1959.

Funkenstein, Amos. *Theology and the Scientific Imagination*. Princeton: Princeton University Press, 1986.

Germino, Dante. "The Contemporary Relevance of the Classics of Political Philosophy." In *Handbook of Political Science*, ed. Fred I. Greenstein and Nelson W. Polsby. Reading, Mass.: Addison-Wesley, 1975.

Gilbert, Felix, ed. *The Historical Essays of Otto Hintze*. New York: Oxford University Press, 1975.

Goldie, Mark. "John Locke and Anglican Royalism." *Political Studies* 31 (1983), 86–102.

Green, T. H. *Hume and Locke*. Ed. Ramon Lemos. New York: Crowell, 1968.

Gutman, Amy. *Democratic Education*. Princeton: Princeton University Press, 1987.

Hartz, Louis. *The Liberal Tradition in America*. New York: Harcourt Brace, 1955.

Hayek, Friedrich. *Law, Legislation and Liberty*, vol. 1: *Rules and Order*. Chicago: University of Chicago Press, 1973.

——. *Law, Legislation and Liberty*, vol. 2: *The Mirage of Social Justice*. Chicago: University of Chicago Press, 1978.

Hill, Christopher. *Writing and Revolution in Seventeenth-Century England*. Amherst: University of Massachusetts Press, 1985.

Hirschman, Albert. *The Passions and the Interests: Political Arguments for Capitalism before Its Triumph*. Princeton: Princeton University Press, 1977.

Hobbes, Thomas. *The English Works*. Ed. Sir William Molesworth. London: J. Bohn, 1839.

——. *Leviathan*. Ed. C. B. Macpherson. New York: Penguin, 1968.

Holmes, Stephen. "The Secret History of Self-Interest." In *Beyond Self-Interest*, Ed. Jane Mansbridge. Chicago: University of Chicago Press, 1990.

Huizinga, Johan. *The Waning of the Middle Ages*. Garden City, N.Y.: Doubleday, 1954.

Hume, David. *Social Contract: Essays by Locke, Hume and Rousseau*. Ed. Ernest Barker. Galaxy Edition. New York: Oxford University Press, 1948.

Hundert, E. J. "The Making of Homo-Faber: John Locke between Ideology and History." *Journal of the History of Ideas* 33, no. 1 (1972), 3–22.

Kateb, George, "Democratic Individuality and the Claims of Politics." *Political Theory* 12 (August 1984), 331–60.

Koyré, Alexandre. "Newton and Descartes." In *Newtonian Studies*. Cambridge: Harvard University Press, 1965.

Kymlicka, Will. *Liberalism, Community, and Culture*. Oxford: Clarendon Press, 1989.

Laplanche, Jean. "Formation of Fantasy." In *Formation of Fantasy*, ed. Victor Burgin, James Donald, and Cora Kaplan. London: Methuen, 1986.

Laski, Harold. *Political Thought in England: From Locke to Bentham*. London: Oxford University Press, 1950.

Leites, Edmund, *The Puritan Conscience and Modern Sexuality*. New Haven: Yale University Press, 1986.

Locke, John. *An Early Draft of Locke's Essay Together with Excerpts from His Journal*. Ed. Richard Ithamar Aaron and Jocelyn Gibb. Oxford: Clarendon Press, 1936.

——. *Locke's Travels in France, 1675–1679*. Ed. John Gough. Cambridge: Cambridge University Press, 1953.

——. *Essays on the Law of Nature*. Ed. W. von Leyden. Oxford: Clarendon Press, 1958.

——. *John Locke on Education*. Ed. Peter Gay. New York: Columbia University, Bureau of Publications, Teacher's College, 1964.

——. *Two Treatises of Government* 2d ed. Ed. Peter Laslett. Cambridge: Cambridge University Press, 1967.

——. *Of the Conduct of the Understanding*. Ed. F. W. Garforth. New York: Columbia University, Teacher's College, 1966.

——. *Two Tracts on Government*. Ed. Philip Abrams. Cambridge: Cambridge University Press, 1967.

——. *Some Thoughts Concerning Education*. Ed. James Axtell. Cambridge: Cambridge University Press, 1968.

——. *An Essay Concerning Human Understanding*. Ed. Peter H. Nidditch. Oxford: Oxford University Press, 1975.

——. *A Letter on Toleration*. Indianapolis: Bobbs-Merrill, 1980.

———. *The Reasonableness of Christianity.* Ed. I. T. Ramsey. Stanford: Stanford University Press, 1989.

McClure, Kirstie M. "Difference, Diversity, and the Limits of Toleration." *Political Theory* 18, no. 3 (1990), 361–91.

Macedo, Stephen. *Liberal Virtues.* Oxford: Oxford University Press, 1990.

Macpherson, C. B. *Political Theory of Possessive Individualism.* Oxford: Oxford University Press, 1962.

Mansbridge, Jane, ed. *Beyond Self-Interest.* Chicago: University of Chicago Press, 1990.

Mansfield, Harvey C., Jr. "Hobbes and the Science of Indirect Government." *American Political Science Review* 65 (1971), 79–110.

Mehta, Uday S. "Liberal Strategies of Exclusion." *Politics and Society* 18, no.4 (1990), 427–54.

Mill, John Stuart. *Essays on Literature and Society.* Ed. J. B. Schneewind. New York: Collier Books, 1965.

———. *Three Essays.* Oxford: Oxford University Press, 1984.

Milton, John. *Paradise Lost: Complete Poems and Major Prose.* Ed. M. Y. Hughes. New York: Odyssey Press, 1957.

Mouffe, Chantal, and Ernesto Laclau. *Hegemony and Socialist Strategy: Towards a Radical Democratic Politics.* New York: Verso, 1985.

Nietzsche, Friedrich. *Basic Writings.* Trans. Walter Kaufmann. New York: Random House, 1966.

———. *Beyond Good and Evil: Prelude to a Philosophy of The Future,* New York: Vintage, 1966.

———. *On the Genealogy of Morals.* Trans. Walter Kaufmann. New York: Random House, 1969.

Norton, Anne. *Reflections on Political Identity.* Baltimore: Johns Hopkins University Press, 1988.

Nozick, Robert. *Anarchy, State and Utopia.* New York: Oxford University Press, 1980.

Oakeshott, Michael. *Rationalism in Politics.* London: Methuen, 1962.

Oestreich, Gerhard. *Neostoicism and the Early Modern State.* Ed. Brigitta Oestreich and H. G. Koenigsberger. Trans. David McLintock. Cambridge: Cambridge University Press, 1982.

Paden, William. "Theatres of Humility and Suspicion: Desert Saints and New England Puritans." In *Technologies of the Self,* ed. Luther H. Martin, Huck Gutman, and Patrick H. Hutton. Amherst: University of Massachusetts Press, 1988.

Pangle, Thomas. *The Spirit of Modern Republicanism.* Chicago: University of Chicago Press, 1988.

Parry, Geraint. "Individuality, Politics and the Critique of Paternalism in John Locke." *Political Studies* 12, no. 2 (1964), 163–77.

Pateman, Carol. *The Sexual Contract.* Stanford: Stanford University Press, 1988.

Patey, Douglas. *Probability and Literary Form: Philosophic Theory and Literary Practice in the Augustan Age.* Cambridge: Cambridge University Press, 1984.

Pitkin, Hanna. *The Concept of Representation.* Berkeley: University of California Press, 1972.

Pocock, J. G. A. *Politics, Language and Time.* New York: Atheneum, 1973.

Quintana, Ricardo. *Two Augustans.* Madison: University of Wisconsin Press, 1978.

Rorty, Richard. *Philosophy and the Mirror of Nature.* Princeton: Princeton University Press, 1979.

Rosenblum, Nancy. *Another Liberalism.* Cambridge: Harvard University Press, 1987.

Rowen, Herbert H. "A Second Thought on Locke's First Treatise." *Journal of the History of Ideas* 17 (1956), 132.

Sallis, John. "Imagination and Presentation in Hegel's Philosophy of Spirit." In *Hegel's Philosophy of Spirit*, ed. Peter G. Stillman. Albany: State University of New York Press, 1987.

Sandel, Michael. *Liberalism and the Limits of Justice.* Cambridge: Cambridge University Press, 1982.

Santayana, George. *Character and Opinion in the United States.* New York: Scribner's, 1924.

Sartre, Jean-Paul. *Being and Nothingness.* Trans. Hazel E. Barnes. New York: Washington Square Press, 1966.

———. *The Psychology of the Imagination.* London: Methuen, 1972.

Schochet, Gordon. *Patriarchalism in Political Thought.* New York: Basic Books, 1975.

Schouls, Peter A. *The Imposition of Method.* Oxford: Clarendon Press, 1980.

Seliger, Martin. *The Liberal Politics of John Locke.* London: Allen and Unwin, 1908.

Sellars, Wilfrid. *Science, Perception, and Reality.* New York: Humanities Press: 1963.

Shapiro, Ian. *The Evolution of Rights in Liberal Theory.* New York: Cambridge University Press, 1986.

Shklar, Judith. Review of *Sources of the Self. Political Theory* 19, no. 1 (February 1991), 105–9.

Simmel, Georg. "Fashion," and "Subordination and Personal Fulfillment." In *On Individuality and Social Forms*, ed. Donald N. Levine. Chicago: University of Chicago Press, 1971.

Spacks, Patricia Meyer. *Imagining a Self: Autobiography and Novel in Eighteenth Century England*. Cambridge: Harvard University Press, 1976.

Strauss, Leo. *Natural Right and History*. Chicago: University of Chicago Press, 1953.

Tarcov, Nathan. *Locke's Education for Liberty*. Chicago: University of Chicago Press, 1984.

Tarlton, Charles D. "A Rope of Sand: Interpreting Locke's *First Treatise on Government*." *Historical Journal* 21, no. 1 (1978), 43–73.

Taylor, Charles. *Philosophy and the Human Sciences: Philosophic Papers*. Cambridge: Cambridge University Press, 1985.

——. *Sources of the Self: The Making of the Modern Identity*. Cambridge: Harvard University Press, 1989.

Thompson, E. P. "Time, Work-Discipline and Industrial Capitalism." *Past and Present* 38 (December 1967), 56–97.

Tocqueville, Alexis de. *Democracy in America*. Trans. G. Lawrence. New York: Anchor Books, 1969.

Trilling, Lionel. *The Liberal Imagination*. New York: Doubleday, Anchor Books, 1950.

Tully, James. "Governing Conduct." In *Conscience and Casuistry in Early Modern Europe*, ed. Edward Leites. Cambridge: Cambridge University Press, 1986.

Tuveson, Ernest. *The Imagination as a Means of Grace: Locke and the Aesthetics of Romanticism*. Berkeley: University of California Press, 1960.

Walzer, Michael. *The Revolution of the Saints*. Cambridge: Harvard University Press, 1965.

Weber, Max. *The Protestant Ethic and the Spirit of Capitalism*. Trans. Talcott Parsons. New York: Charles Scribner's Sons, 1958.

——. *Economy and Society*. Ed. Guenther Roth and Claus Wittich. Berkeley: University of California Press, 1978.

Weinreb, Lloyd. *Natural Law and Justice*. Cambridge: Harvard University Press, 1987.

Williams, Bernard. *Moral Luck*. Cambridge: Cambridge University Press, 1981.

Wolin, Sheldon. *Politics and Vision: Continuity and Innovation in Western Political Thought*. Boston: Little, Brown, 1960.

——. "Political Theory as a Vocation." *American Political Science Review* 63, no. 4 (1969), 1062–82.

Yolton, John. *John Locke and the Way of Ideas*. Oxford: Oxford University Press, 1956.

Index